DATE DUE

OC 9 '96			
OC 30 '96			
RENEW			
DE 2 96			
JY 26 05			
AP 18 06			
MY 25 06			

DEMCO 38-296

HIROHITO AND HIS TIMES

HIROHITO
AND HIS TIMES

A JAPANESE PERSPECTIVE

Toshiaki Kawahara
Introduction • W. G. Beasley

KODANSHA INTERNATIONAL
Tokyo and New York

Distributed in the United States by Kodansha International/USA Ltd., through Farrar, Straus and Giroux, Publishers, 19 Union Square West, New York 10003.

Published by Kodansha International Ltd., 17-14 Otowa 1-chome, Bunkyo-ku, Tokyo 112 and Kodansha International/USA Ltd., 114 5th Avenue, New York, New York 10011.

ISBN 4-7700-1479-1 C0021 (Japan)
ISBN 0-87011-979-6 (USA)
First edition, 1990

Library of Congress Cataloging-in-Publication Data

Kawahara, Toshiaki, 1921-
   Hirohito and His Times: A Japanese Perspective/ by Toshiaki Kawahara; Introduction by W. G. Beasley.
   1. Hirohito, Emperor of Japan, 1901-1989, 2. Japan—Emperors—Biography.
3. Japan—History—Shōwa Period, 1926-1989. I. Title.
DS889.8.K389 1990
952.03'3'092—dc20

89-77698

CONTENTS

INTRODUCTION by W. G. Beasley   vii

PROLOGUE: A Farewell to Shōwa   1

Part One: Early Years

New Century, Old Ways   9

Imperial Studies   23

Coming of Age   35

Part Two: The Emperor at War

The Limits of Power   49

Patriots and Soldiers   63

The First Shot   81

Hirohito at Home   90

"A Strange and Complex Situation"   97

War in the Pacific   113

"Your Majesty's Counsel"   124

Part Three: The Emperor's Peace

Another Emperor Outside the Moat   139

Friends and Enemies   149

Riding Out the Storm   164
The Crown Prince's Bride   175
Symbol of the New Japan   187
Behind the Chrysanthemum Curtain   200

Prime Ministers and Cabinets, 1912–1989   210
Index   212

INTRODUCTION

In 1873 Japan adopted the Gregorian calendar to replace the lunar calendar, originally taken from China, which had been in use since the seventh century. From that time on, the Japanese year and its subdivision into weeks and months came into line with Western practice. But the numbering of the years themselves remained traditional: That is to say, each year was identified serially by its place within an "era" corresponding to an emperor's reign. The era had a name, chosen to be auspicious, which subsequently became the emperor's posthumous title. Thus, when Hirohito came to the throne in 1926, that became the first year of Shōwa (Illustrious Harmony, or Illustrious Peace), and when he died in 1989, the Shōwa era came to an end in its sixty-fourth year. Hirohito will be known in future history books as the Shōwa Emperor.

The everyday habits of such a system of dating have helped to enhance the Japanese people's awareness of their emperor's role in national life. On the other hand, it has encouraged the use of oversimplified labels. To suggest that

"Shōwa history" has a kind of coherence or unity, other than that which derives from being the record of Hirohito's reign, is misleading. The first twenty years of the period saw an economic slump (1929–30), followed by the rise of militarism, expansion in Asia, and the Pacific War. Defeat then brought military occupation by the victors, who carried out far-reaching reforms of Japanese political and social institutions (including the reform of the monarchy), which proved to be the prelude to both parliamentary democracy and rapid economic growth. Hirohito therefore reigned during two very different phases of Japanese history.

The part he himself played in them has been a matter of controversy. On the one hand there are those, both in Japan and elsewhere in the world, who have attributed to him a measure of war guilt as great as that which attached to the members of prewar and wartime cabinets. As a theoretically absolute monarch, it is argued, he was responsible for what was done in his name: the decision to prosecute the war in the first place, as well as the actions, including the atrocities, that were carried out during it. Others maintain, equally vociferously, that because he lacked the means effectively to intervene, and was even precluded by his constitutional position from trying to do so, that charge cannot be sustained.

A second element of controversy concerns precisely the question of his constitutional position. Although there may well have been a time in the distant past when Japanese emperors ruled as well as reigned, for a thousand years or more before the nineteenth century they did no more than preside over a government that was openly controlled by aristocrats or feudal lords. Then—as matters are seen by the majority of Japanese historians, though not of conservative politicians—during the reign of Hirohito's grandfather, the Meiji Emperor, which lasted from 1868 to 1912, the monarch became part of a system of government that was both absolutist and bureaucratic. This not only subordinated popular liberties and the welfare of the people to the needs of an accelerated program of modernization, designed to make Japan internationally strong, but also opened the way to the militarism and fascism on which it is possible to lay the blame for Japan's twentieth-century imperialism and aggression. In other words, the "emperor system," as it is called, is said to be at the heart of Japan's prewar ills. Although Hirohito had no share in devising it, he was its latest representative and defender. For this reason he is touched by its guilt.

In this context, too, there is a counter-argument. It goes back to the nature of the monarchy as established by the Meiji Constitution of 1889, and several decisions associated with it. The constitution had two principal characteristics. One of these was the incorporation of a range of European-style provisions, especially German ones, to create a framework for modern Japanese government, in which the appointed executive would be strong and the elected legislature would be weak. The other lay in the clauses that gave legitimacy to the document by reference to the emperor's supposedly divine descent from the sun goddess, Amaterasu, rather than by an appeal to social theory. The constitution was officially held to be the emperor's gift to his people. He was bound by it only because he chose to do so. This made him theoretically absolute, in that the constitution recognized no higher authority (except that of his ancestors, perhaps). Against that, he was not provided with any mechanism by which to intervene in the day-to-day running of the state. He did not preside over the cabinet, for example. Ordinances issued in his name had to be countersigned by a minister. As a result, his role became by convention that of responding to the recommendations of the powerful men who composed the executive branch of government. If they were agreed on what to recommend, it was assumed that he would approve it. If not, he had an element of choice.

Hirohito inherited this order of things more or less intact from a father who was both politically weak and mentally ill. At first it posed no great problems. The political parties, reflecting for the most part the interests of commercial and industrial enterprises, were growing in influence in the 1920s, but insofar as they sought to bring about institutional reform, their object of attack was the bureaucracy, rather than the monarchy. All this changed after 1930, however. The men who competed for power thereafter—that is, the military and the nationalists who supported them—conceived of a "purified" political structure, based on a more direct relationship between the emperor and his people, in which parliament, industrialists, and liberals of every kind would be set aside. The result was to bring the monarchy inescapably to the forefront of politics. It was not supposed that the emperor himself would have to do anything very different from what he had always done. Nevertheless, there would be new groups speaking in his name, new policies to be ratified by his authority, and a new interpretation of the constitution to be imposed upon his subjects. This implied that if the emperor and his immediate advisers clung to received wisdom about the nature of the Meiji Constitution, they were likely to provoke domestic confrontation. They proved unwilling to do so.

The potential conflict between court and cabinet was resolved in 1935 and 1936. Late in 1935 a campaign of public criticism was mounted by nationalists against the emperor's advisers and their political attitudes. Early in 1936 army officers attempted a coup d'état, seizing the center of Tokyo for several days. Out of these events came compromise, made possible in part by Hirohito's own firmness in the face of the rebels. Court circles, notably the elder statesman Kinmochi Saionji, accepted that there would have to be a radical redirection of Japanese policy, both at home and abroad, and gave up any serious attempt to prevent it from taking place. They concentrated thereafter on the long-term goal of keeping the monarchy intact. The less radical elements in the army and navy, together with their civilian allies, contented themselves for their part with control of essential policies shorn of constitutional revision. Unlike contemporary Germany and Italy, Japan therefore carried forward into the age of the Second World War a political system that had a large measure of continuity with that of the nineteenth century.

It is in this context that one needs to set the events of 1941 and 1945. The final Japanese decisions leading to war were taken at imperial conferences—that is, meetings of senior members of the cabinet and armed forces—held in the presence of the emperor. There is evidence that Hirohito expressed uneasiness at what was being proposed, but he did so in the form of questions about practicality and prospects of success, making no obvious effort to force substantial reconsideration. Accordingly, there is nothing in the record to suggest that he can be held free of responsibility for what was done. By contrast, when Japan faced defeat in 1945, similar meetings to consider the possibilities of surrender reached deadlock, which was broken only by the emperor's personal intervention on the side of peace (after the dropping of the atom bombs on Hiroshima and Nagasaki). It is in the light of these facts that postwar apologists—including Hirohito on one occasion—have argued that his actions were in accordance with constitutional practice: accepting an agreed recommendation from his ministers in 1941; intervening when they were unable to reach an agreement in 1945.

What is lacking in the debate that this has occasioned is convincing evidence of Hirohito's own ideas and views. Statements made by his close advisers, who were in the best position to know, are suspect, because they were made after surrender, when the question of whether to put the emperor on trial as a war criminal had already been raised. Official records are incomplete, many having been deliberately destroyed (although one cannot be sure that any of these concerned the throne). In short, it remains a great deal easier to write about the monarchy at this time than about Hirohito as a person.

For different reasons this is also true of the period after the war came to an end. Despite pressure from Russia, Australia, and a number of Asian countries, a decision was taken by the American government in 1945 to preserve the monarchy and leave Hirohito on the throne. In essence this was because of a belief that to do otherwise might make

Japan ungovernable, at least by an occupation force of any reasonable size, but this did not prevent the introduction of reforms that fundamentally changed the nature of imperial rule. At the beginning of 1946 the palace was required to issue a New Year's rescript rejecting "the false conception that the emperor is divine." In the postwar constitution, which came into force in 1947, he became instead "a symbol of the state."

A fresh generation of imperial advisers took this as the framework for greatly modifying the part that the emperor played in public life. In a disarmed and studiously democratic Japan there was no place for military ceremonial in which he could participate. Nor was there much by way of civil ceremony of an ostentatious kind. And it was in any case judged best that the monarch should adopt a low profile after the sharp controversies of 1945–46. Later, once the peace treaty had been signed, there were visits to America and Europe, but these aroused enough signs of hostility to suggest that it would not be wise to put the emperor into a prominent position internationally. That left very little for him to do that was likely to attract public attention. His own taste for scholarship (not only as a marine biologist) and for traditional culture was not the kind of thing to make headlines. For political reasons he had to hold aloof from the reviving nationalism of the 1970s and eighties which prompted visits by government ministers to the principal Shinto shrines. That left him to be presented as the conscientious performer of some ritual duties, and as a quiet family man. Press and television found this unexciting. As a result, the monarchy became acceptable but dull. It was only through the long-drawn-out illness leading to his death, and the ceremony of his funeral, that Hirohito could be said to have caught the imagination of the Japanese people once again.

All this makes Hirohito a difficult subject for biography, a man at once colorless and highly controversial. Yet, the prominence of his place in the history of the twentieth century makes it important to try to form an estimate of him. Few are better able to do so than Toshiaki Kawahara, who has spent much of his adult life as a professional observer of the imperial court, thereby acquiring a fund of knowledge about it and a special expertise in the interpretation of such personal records about the emperor as exist.

W. G. Beasley
Professor Emeritus, University of London

PROLOGUE: A Farewell to Shōwa

The first indication that something was wrong with Emperor Hirohito came during a banquet held to celebrate his eighty-sixth birthday on April 29, 1987. In the middle of the meal he became ill. He recovered quickly, and his doctor assumed that the incident was simply a manifestation of stress and fatigue—not surprising in a man of Hirohito's age. That summer, as he did every year, the emperor went to the imperial villa at Nasu to escape the heat of the city. Located one hundred miles north of Tokyo on an unspoiled plateau, Nasu was an open laboratory where Hirohito could conduct his research in botany. In the weeks that followed, he exhibited a number of disturbing symptoms. Once he fainted after returning from an expedition to collect specimens. He started to vomit at bedtime and passed blood in his stools.

After he returned to Tokyo in mid-September, he underwent an exhaustive medical examination in the palace hospital. His doctors discovered that a tumor in his pancreas was partially blocking his digestive tract. Since the likelihood of cancer was high, they argued for the immediate removal of the obstruction. Palace officials, however, opposed surgery on the grounds that no doctor had ever before touched an emperor with a scalpel and removed part of his body. Until the end of the Meiji era, the emperor's body was considered sacred, and could not be touched by ordinary people. When a doctor wanted to take the emperor's pulse, he had to stretch a silk thread across his patient's wrist.

Hirohito's condition was clearly grave, however, and it was obvious that anything less than major surgery would result in his early death. In the end, the argument was settled by asking the emperor himself to give his consent to the operation.

The palace's permanent medical staff consisted of three cardiologists and one gastrointestinal specialist. It was thought that such a team would be able to deal with any emergency—especially a heart attack or stroke—that might affect the emperor or empress. On this occasion, however, the surgeon chosen for the operation was not a member of the palace team. The procedure called for a specialist in the kind of condition afflicting the emperor, and the palace chose Dr. Yasuhiko Morioka, the head of Tokyo University Hospital. Although Dr. Morioka was advised of the situation six days before the scheduled operation, he did not examine his patient or even see his medical records until the day itself. In other words, he went into the operating theater unprepared.

This may seem a shocking lack of concern, but there were reasons. Dr. Morioka was fifty-seven years old. He had been brought up to believe that the emperor was a living

2

god. To be introduced to the emperor, let alone to be asked to operate on him, was beyond his wildest imagination. There was no telling what horrible mistake he might make if his hands began to shake during the operation. The palace felt that it would be better for Dr. Morioka's composure if he did not meet his patient beforehand.

The precaution worked perfectly. Dr. Morioka came through the four-hour operation calm and composed. As it turned out, the tumor had been very difficult to reach, and the merest slip on the surgeon's part might have proved fatal for Hirohito. The operation confirmed that the tumor was cancerous. However, following Japanese medical practice, the gravity of his condition was kept from Hirohito, who was told, as was the nation, that he was suffering from "chronic pancreatitis."

After the operation, Hirohito's health seemed to improve. His appetite returned, he began to regain his color, and he even resumed some of the official duties he had entrusted to the crown prince during his illness. But the reprieve was only temporary. A year after the operation, he began to bleed internally, and subsequently he required frequent, and then almost constant, blood transfusions. The end came at 6:33 A.M. on January 7, 1989. Hirohito was eighty-seven years and nine months old.

***

Hirohito's state funeral was held in Tokyo in a specially constructed funeral hall in the Shinjuku Imperial Gardens. On the morning of February 24, the funeral cortege left the imperial palace at 9:30 A.M. The hearse was preceded by an honor guard of thirty-two motorcyclists and followed by thirty-eight cars, forming a motorcade 1,000 meters long. Sixty-two years before, at the funeral of Hirohito's father, Emperor Taishō, the hearse had been drawn by four oxen, and 4,000 mourners, including the imperial family and Japanese and foreign dignitaries, had walked the same six-kilometer route to Shinjuku.

The customs of the imperial house dictate that an emperor should be buried at night, but on this occasion security ruled out both the antique hearse and the nighttime services. The funeral was held during the day, and unfortunately it was a cold, drizzly day—the coldest of that winter.

As a court musician played the traditional dirge on the koto, Emperor Akihito stood in front of the bier, raised a Shinto prayer wand and spoke this simple eulogy: "I, Akihito, humbly offer these words to the spirit of my departed father, the Shōwa Emperor. Since you passed away, our sorrow has known no bounds. Your kindly face still appears before our eyes, and we shall never be able to forget you."

The emperor bowed reverently before withdrawing. Once the other members of the imperial family had paid their last respects, the private part of the funeral was over. During a ten-minute interval, a curtain was drawn between the funeral hall and the mourners' tents to screen the removal of the Shinto cult objects, the plain wooden gate, and the *sakaki* trees that were used in the first part of the ceremony. The need for a private religious ceremony was occasioned by the clause in Japan's postwar constitution that forbids the state from engaging in any form of religious

4

activity. The imperial family practice Shinto, and a public religious ceremony, financed by taxpayers' money, would have violated the constitution. The compromise reached by the Imperial Household Agency and the government was to hold two separate ceremonies: the first, private and religious, and the second, public and secular.

After one minute of silence, Prime Minister Noboru Takeshita delivered a brief message of condolence. He was followed by Japanese dignitaries and the representatives of 164 countries and 28 international organizations. The ceremony lasted a little more than an hour. The emperor's remains were then taken by car to be interred next to his father, Emperor Taishō, in the Musashino Imperial Mausoleum.

The remarkable thing about Hirohito's funeral was that almost every country sent representatives. What speaks even more clearly of Japan's position in the world was the presence of fifty-five heads of state, including President George Bush of the United States and President François Mitterand of France. Yet, at the same time, in Great Britain, Australia, the Netherlands, New Zealand, China, Korea, and Singapore, there was considerable debate about whom to send to the funeral. Many of Japan's former enemies in World War II were unable or unwilling to grieve for a man whom they held responsible for the loss of so many lives and for so much suffering. In an article headlined "No Tears for Evil Lord of Japan," one British newspaper wrote: "Hirohito died unpunished for his part in some of the most heinous crimes ever inflicted on mankind." (*The Sun,* 1989).

The bitterness of the article shocked many Japanese. But

there was worse to come. New Zealand's defense minister, Bob Tizard, was even blunter: "Hirohito should have been shot immediately after the war; executed with eight bullets in a public square. And we should have sent representatives to the execution."

Under these circumstances, several countries did not send their heads of state. Great Britain sent Queen Elizabeth's consort, Prince Philip; the Netherlands and China sent their foreign ministers; and South Korea, its premier.

When Prince Philip approached the bier, he did not bow, but just stared at it for a few moments before withdrawing. The next day, he traveled to Yokohama and visited the graves of British and Commonwealth servicemen who had died during the war.

PART ONE:

EARLY YEARS

New Century, Old Ways

April 29, 1901. The skies, which had been overcast since morning, began to clear by evening. Majestic sunset clouds trailed across the sky, which gradually darkened and filled with stars. The crown prince's palace, until then hushed and still, was suddenly thrown into uproar: Crown Prince Yoshihito's consort, Sadako, had gone into labor. The young couple had been married almost a year, and the nation eagerly awaited the birth of their first child.

At 10:10 P.M., the strained atmosphere of the birth chamber was shattered by the cry of a healthy newborn, a cry that reached the ears of the court doctor in the adjoining room. He was filled with a sense of relief, yet at the same time held his breath: Was the baby a new prince or a new princess?

The door opened and a smiling court lady announced proudly, "It's a prince!"

The baby boy was Hirohito, the Shōwa Emperor, one hundred twenty-fourth in an unbroken line of Japanese sovereigns and one of a mere handful whose names are readily called to mind. How did he come by his name? Shortly after his birth, a committee of scholars was convened to choose two names for the newborn—an imperial name and a princely name—from ancient Chinese books. In one of these, the *Han Shu* by Ban Gu, they found the following passage: "If the country is *affluent*, the people will be at peace." *Hiro,* the Chinese character that means "affluent," was chosen as the first character of his imperial name. *Hito,* meaning "humane; generous; humanity," became the second character, in accordance with a custom going back more than 1,000 years which held that it should be used in the names of the highest-ranking imperial princes. His princely name was Michinomiya.

After the names were selected, the baby's father, Crown Prince Yoshihito, wrote the name Hirohito with brush and ink, while the imperial household minister did the same with the princely name Michinomiya. These papers were laid at the pillow of the newborn child. Then the names were formally announced in the three Shinto shrines on the palace grounds. Customarily, the naming ceremony is performed seven days after the birth. In Hirohito's case, it fell on May 5, the day of the Boy's Festival, a traditional celebration offering health and prosperity to all male children.

For the first few weeks of his life, Hirohito was nursed by his mother and a wet nurse at the crown prince's palace. The wet nurse took responsibility for the prince at night or when the mother was away. Imperial wet nurses were chosen only after a rigorous investigation of their characters, their general health (they must have no history of hereditary illnesses), and the quality and quantity of their milk.

***

The Japan of Hirohito's birth was far removed from the isolated, backward realm inherited by his grandfather, Emperor Meiji, thirty-three years before. At the turn of the century, Japan's national prestige was on the rise, and its economy prospered under modern industrial capitalism. Japan's modernization, however, was not entirely a peaceful enterprise. The Meiji government, fearing that Japan might suffer the same fate as the Chinese empire, which had been forced to sign unequal commercial treaties with the Western powers, pursued a policy of "strengthening the army and enriching the country." Japan's fledgling industries needed raw materials and foreign markets, and its growing population more land to relieve the pressure on the archipelago's four small islands. In the nineteenth century, trade disputes were usually settled by warfare. In 1840 the British had fought a war to protect their lucrative opium trade with China. Following the example of their European and American mentors, the Japanese began to look overseas for commercial and military opportunities of their own.

In 1894, Japan had gone to war with China over Korea, then nominally a vassal state of the Ching dynasty. The tiny island nation startled the world by defeating the "sleeping lion of China" in under two years. A decade later, Japan upset the century-old Western domination of Asia by challenging a European power: On February 10, 1904,

11

Japan declared war on Russia. The origins of the conflict went back to the Boxer Rebellion of 1900–1901, during which antiforeign Chinese insurgents were put down by a joint expeditionary force of European, American, and Japanese troops. As part of the action, the Russians stationed a large number of soldiers in Manchuria; yet, once the rebellion was over, they refused to withdraw. This violated their treaty with China, but not only did they ignore that fact, they also made it clear they had designs on Korea, which Japan considered to be within its own sphere of influence.

Russian ambitions in Manchuria and Korea posed a threat that could not be ignored. The two sides tried and failed to reach a negotiated settlement. With its fortunes as a nation at stake, Japan was forced to take action. The Anglo-Japanese Alliance, concluded in 1902, provided excellent protection; the British had their own economic interests in India and China to protect and did not want to see the Russians move south.

The Japanese scored major victories against the Russians on the battlefields of Manchuria, but it was their success at sea that caught the world's attention. On May 27 and 28, 1905, the combined Japanese fleet, commanded by Admiral Tōgō, virtually wiped out the Russian Baltic fleet, which had sailed half way around the world to meet the enemy in the Sea of Japan. The Japanese sank twenty-one Russian ships, captured seven, and took the Russian commander in chief prisoner. The victory rivaled Nelson's destruction of the French and Spanish fleets at the Battle of Trafalgar a century before.

In January 1905, uprisings that would lead to the revolution hampered Russia's ability to wage war; Japan, too, was sorely overstretched. The two sides accepted the mediation of President Theodore Roosevelt and signed the Treaty of Portsmouth three and a half months after the decisive sea battle.

Although Japan had won, the treaty did not provide for an indemnity, and this stirred dissatisfaction at home, which escalated into rioting. Nevertheless, victories over China and Russia in just ten years propelled Japan into the ranks of the world powers. At the same time, however, the hubris and pride that went along with these victories spawned a reckless drive toward imperialistic expansionism. Many Japanese believed that the country needed colonies of its own to match its new prestige. Naturally, this caused friction between Japan and its neighbors, particularly the Chinese, and put Japan in danger of being shunned by the rest of the world.

***

Seventy days after his birth, Prince Hirohito was separated from his family and sent to another household to be raised. This had been a common practice among the imperial family and the upper aristocracy for centuries. There were numerous examples of children dying in mysterious circumstances as a result of the rivalries among the ladies of the household, which is perhaps the main reason the custom had persisted. Children could also be a hindrance in the home of an important family, and the polygamous nature of such households did not make them the ideal environment in which to bring up a child.

Hirohito was to be entrusted to a family of good lineage with a military background, and one in which husband and wife were in excellent health. The first to be approached was General Ōyama. Although he was a distinguished career officer, he declined. And, indeed, the responsibility was enormous. Just the worries alone would be a burden, and if the child got sick or, worse yet, died, the general knew he might have to be prepared to commit suicide. The next choice was Count Sumiyoshi Kawamura, a retired vice-admiral in the Japanese navy. Kawamura was descended from a samurai family in Satsuma, an area of Kyushu famed for the valor of its fighters. He had served three times as navy minister, and was well respected for his integrity and devotion to duty.

At New Year's in 1901, before Hirohito was even born, Crown Prince Yoshihito had spoken to Count Kawamura personally. "An imperial baby is soon to be born. We do not know whether it will be a boy or a girl, but I would like to have you raise the child, thinking of him or her as your own. . . ."

The elderly officer was deeply moved and accepted. The Kawamuras must have felt both nervous and proud, preparing to take on responsibility for the child that would one day ascend the throne of Japan.

On July 7, Prince Hirohito arrived at the Kawamura villa, to take up residence in a separate pavilion that had been built for him in the garden. His new home was in Azabu, about two kilometers south of the crown prince's palace. Joining the prince in shifts at the Kawamura home were a doctor and nurse from the palace medical staff, as well as his wet nurse. The count's wife and his eldest daughter also served Hirohito day and night.

To the delight of the imperial family, on June 25, 1902, a second son, Prince Chichibu, was born to the crown prince and his consort. Chichibu was also entrusted to the Kawamura family to be raised with his older brother. Unfortunately, the kind but aging Count Kawamura had not much longer to live. He died on August 12, 1904. The emotional shock must have been great for the three-year-old Prince Hirohito, for whom Kawamura had been like a real father. The count's widow petitioned to be relieved of her guardianship over the two princes, who were moved on November 9 to a newly built residence in Akasaka.

In the spring of 1906, a special kindergarten was set up for Prince Hirohito and Prince Chichibu on the grounds of the crown prince's residence. It consisted of three twelve-foot-by-twelve-foot adjoining tatami-mat rooms. The sliding panels that separated them were removed to form one large space. Cotton cushions were wrapped around the pillars so that even if the children bumped into them they would not get hurt. Five children from the noblest families were selected as companions for the royal offspring. The five were all one year older than Hirohito, the hope being that they would speed his intellectual development.

This was the first time Hirohito had come into contact with other children his own age, and while it was presumably beneficial from the standpoint of his personality development, there is no doubt that he found it hard to get close to others. He was by nature introverted and reticent, generally uncomfortable around people. Chamberlain Count Kanroji wrote of the young Hirohito:

The young Prince Hirohito was not particularly well

coordinated. It even took him a long time to do up the buttons on his Western-style clothes. It was most irritating to stand by and watch him, and one wanted to reach out and help. But one could only stand there patiently, and the more one stared at him the more he fumbled. We have the expression "twice more than others," but for His Majesty, it was "three times more."

In contrast, Hirohito's younger brother, Prince Chichibu, was confident and outgoing and became the "leader" of the group. Kanroji had more to say about Hirohito at this age: "He looked frail and serious in his youth, never smiling or laughing. He did not appear to take any joy in either exercise or play." When he fell down, his aides would rush to his side and pick him up. When, following the lead of the other children, he tried jumping from a wall, his attendants were there to catch him. It appears that this overprotectiveness served only to dull his motor skills and sense of self-reliance, and fostered a dependent quality in him.

After two years in this kindergarten, Prince Hirohito was ready to enter elementary school. It was during his first year at the Peers' School that he met a man whom he was to respect and love for the rest of his life: General Maresuke Nogi. Nogi was an exemplar of *bushidō*, the traditional way of the samurai. As commander of the Third Army during the Russo-Japanese War, he had led his troops into the attack on 203-Meter Hill, a supposedly impregnable Russian stronghold which the Japanese took after bitter fighting. Although his two sons had died in the assault, he treated the defeated Russian commander most graciously. He was first and always a military man, with no taste for politics. Emperor Meiji had personally appointed Nogi as principal of the Peers' School, indicating how dissatisfied he had been with the school as it was then. Himself a man of great integrity, the emperor saw the Peers' School as little more than a place for rich, pampered children. From that standpoint, General Nogi was the perfect choice to be its new head. Believing that, in order to effect change at the school, the principal himself should be a model, Nogi moved out of his Akasaka villa and into the plain headmaster's residence on the school campus.

The school's elementary division was in Yotsuya, a few minutes' walk across the street from the grounds of the crown prince's palace. When Hirohito got out of school each day, General Nogi would always be there at the gate to see him off. Hirohito would salute the uniformed headmaster, who would invariably straighten the young prince's cap, adjust the angle of his salute, or give him advice on some matter or other. Once a week, Nogi would invite Hirohito to his office and tell him instructive military stories, or teach him about the comportment expected of an emperor.

In those days, elementary school students treated their teachers and the school principal with the utmost respect. The Ministry of Education required its teachers to develop a remote persona, which established a distance between teacher and student and inspired a kind of awe. This system applied even to Hirohito, the "offspring of the gods," and coupled with the fact that Nogi gave him special attention, it is not surprising that a strong bond of mutual respect and esteem developed between them. As an example of how deep Hirohito's respect for Nogi ran, once, when one of Hirohito's companions started to say "The principal. . ." the young prince immediately interrupted him, saying, "You should call him 'His Excellency, the Principal.' "

Yet, "His Excellency, the Principal" could sometimes cause Prince Hirohito some discomfort. From time to time he would visit the classroom where Hirohito was studying and stand in the back of the room to observe the lesson. This inevitably made the prince very nervous, and he would freeze up. In turn, Nogi was well aware of the discomfort he was causing, but he considered it a weakness that had to be corrected. Such character-forming lessons must have been invaluable for the boy who was later to become emperor and commander in chief. It is not easy to change innate personality traits, but even though he was just a child, Hirohito worked hard at it.

***

In the summer of 1912, his fifth year at the Peers' School, Hirohito received two serious emotional shocks. His grandfather, Emperor Meiji, was well known for his distrust of doctors. Much larger than the average Japanese and with a strong constitution, he tended to be overconfident about his own health. He was robust by nature, and he disdained the periodic medical checkups he was supposed to receive from the palace doctors. Whenever they suggested a more comprehensive physical examination, he would dismiss them with a curt "I'm fine."

From 1906 the fifty-three-year-old Emperor Meiji began suffering from diabetes and general kidney failure, but as always, he refused a detailed examination because he did not feel worse than normal. By the spring of 1912 his condition had grown much more serious, but the emperor continued to treat it lightly, paying little attention to his diet.

On July 10, 1912, while attending the graduation ceremonies of Tokyo Imperial University, the emperor suddenly felt very tired and short of breath. This time not even he could turn the doctors away. A thorough examination revealed that uremic poisoning had already set in. In those days such a condition was considered fatal.

Not content with just the court doctors' diagnosis, the palace called in two specialists from the University of Tokyo. There was a problem, however. The two doctors were professors at Japan's leading university, and were among the most prominent experts in their field. Nevertheless, they could not examine the emperor without receiving some sort of court title from the Imperial Household Ministry. Thus, on the morning of July 20, an emergency ceremony was held in which the two were granted the title of "imperial aide" and made official members of the palace bureaucracy. Only then could they attend their patient.

Although it is difficult to imagine now, in those days no one was allowed to give the emperor an injection, no matter how serious his condition. This meant that even the best doctor would be constrained in his treatment, unable to apply modern techniques and thus often unable to take the most appropriate course of action.

On July 20 the palace issued its first public statement confirming that something was wrong with the emperor. The nation was stunned. The Japanese revered virtually as a god this wise and able ruler during whose reign Japan had gone so far in such a short space of time. From early morning till late into the night, people flooded into the plaza in front of the imperial palace and knelt to pray for their sovereign's health. At Shinto shrines throughout the nation, prayers were offered for his recovery. Even the transit authorities in Tokyo cooperated. The rails at Miyakezaka, near the emperor's sickbed in the palace, set up a harsh metallic rasping whenever tramcars went around the curve there, so the cars were asked to slow down, and blankets were packed around the rails to muffle the noise. Also, the guns that were fired each day at noon to mark the time at the palace were moved elsewhere.

The entertainment industry, too, showed restraint out of respect for the emperor. There were no movie houses in those days, but the other kinds of theaters all closed their doors.

But the emperor's condition worsened by the hour, and despite the public's prayers, he passed away at 12:43 A.M. on July 30, 1912. He was fifty-nine years and nine months old. With him ended the brilliant era of Japanese history that bore his name.

The funeral—on an unprecedented scale—was held on the night of September 13 in a funeral hall erected on the Aoyama Parade Grounds. Among those present was Arthur, Duke of Connaught, the younger brother of Britain's King George V. In accordance with custom, the funeral services were scheduled to begin at 10:00 P.M. The carriage bearing the body was pulled (again, as tradition dictated) by four oxen. The procession set out from the Imperial Palace at 7:00 P.M., but it was two hours later before the last members got started. Seven thousand people attended the funeral, while another 300,000 citizens lined the streets to watch the procession.

Following Emperor Meiji's death, his son, Crown Prince Yoshihito, ascended the throne as Emperor Taishō, while Hirohito automatically became crown prince.

***

General Nogi's residence was barely one kilometer from the funeral site in Aoyama. There, on the night before the services, Nogi and his wife committed suicide. In a Japanese-style room of their two-story house, Nogi's wife, Shizuko, was found slumped on the floor where she had been stabbed in the heart with a short sword. Judging from the scene, Nogi had dealt her the fatal blow himself. As for the general, he first cut a horizontal gash in his abdomen and then tried to sever his own head, leaving it partly attached. Those who saw the aftermath described it as a suicide in the traditional manner. General Nogi was a warrior of the old school. When the emperor he had revered died, he could only follow by sacrificing his own life.

The event deeply moved the Japanese, and while many praised it, there were also quite a few who deplored the general's action. *Junshi,* the custom of following one's lord into death, went back to ancient times. A third-century Chinese chronicle describes a nation known as Yamatai (in the Japanese archipelago) and tells that when its empress died, hundreds followed her by committing suicide. The practice continued, and in the Tokugawa period (1603–1868) it became a matter of pride to kill oneself when one's master died. Indeed, such suicides grew so numerous that they were prohibited by the Tokugawa government in 1663. The custom was believed to have died out until General Nogi revived it.

One can imagine the shock and pain Hirohito must have felt when he found out about it the next day. It was cruel news for an eleven-year-old boy to hear that his mentor, the man he had loved and honored like a god and parent combined, had cut himself open and followed Emperor Meiji in death. The young crown prince must have recalled his last meeting with Nogi, just two days before. The general had acted rather strangely that day. At ten o'clock on the morning of the eleventh, he had appeared at Hirohito's residence unkempt, his eyes dull and sunken, without their usual sparkle. He'd always had a full beard, but on that day it was rather untidy. He stood straight and still in front of Hirohito and began explaining to him the military duties of the crown prince. He also gave Hirohito two books, traditional works on the duties of the throne, the important parts of which he had marked in red for the crown prince's benefit, with instructions to have his attendants read the difficult passages to him until he was old enough to read them himself. It was clear that the general had come to bid him farewell.

Imperial Studies

Two or three years before Prince Hirohito was due to finish elementary school, palace officials began to debate the next step in his education. Eventually, those who favored an "imperial education" in a special environment won out. They felt that Hirohito, who was by nature rather awkward and uncoordinated, should not be put in with other children at the very age when they would be most likely to tease him. There were other reasons to isolate Hirohito during his education. In the first decades of the twentieth century, Japan's socialist and democratic movements were gaining strength. In 1911 the nation was rocked by the discovery of an anarchist plot to assassinate Emperor Meiji. Although the plotters were arrested before they could carry out their plan, their aims had sympathizers even among the intellectuals at such aristocratic establishments as the Peers' School. And finally, from the standpoint of security, it would not do to have to worry about several score new children from other schools.

Since General Nogi had supported the idea of a special

educational program for Hirohito, it was decided to establish a separate learning center for the crown prince on the grounds of the Togu Palace. The school was to be headed by Admiral Tōgō, the hero of the Russo-Japanese war, and with top scholars on the teaching staff. Since it was deemed too lonely and not good emotionally for Hirohito to study all by himself, five other students were selected to join him in this "mini-school."

For the next seven years, until March 1921, Crown Prince Hirohito followed a standard junior and senior high school curriculum, except for music, arts and crafts, and composition, which were deemphasized, presumably because he showed little aptitude for them. In their place he received lessons in horseback riding and military science, which were deemed indispensable for the future commander in chief of Japan's armed forces. He also studied French. Ordinary junior high school students studied English, but in those days French was still the language of diplomacy and of the aristocracy.

One subject considered particularly important in this special imperial curriculum was ethics. After a lengthy search, Shigetake Sugiura was appointed to be his tutor in this field. A distinguished scholar of Chinese and ethics, Sugiura had been principal of the Tokyo University Preparatory School, Japan's most prestigious secondary institution. As Hirohito's tutor, Sugiura preferred concrete examples to abstract theories in his lectures. Under his guidance, Hirohito, single-minded if not exactly brilliant, strove to become an unselfish, impartial sovereign. He listened to the lectures with rapt attention, delighting Admiral Tōgō, who sat in on the lessons from time to time.

Sugiura's ideas about imperial ethics had an incalculable impact on Hirohito's intellectual development.

***

Just three months after the crown prince's special classes commenced, World War I broke out. The war started after the assassination of Austria's Archduke Ferdinand in Sarajevo, but its real causes lay in the imperial rivalries of the European powers. The conflict spread to East Asia when England enlisted the help of the Japanese navy in combating German warships off the coast of China. The Japanese were only too pleased to get involved. Not only did they have an alliance with England, they also saw it as an opportunity to enhance their international standing and gain a foothold in China by supplanting German interests there. Thus they sided with the Allies, declaring war on Germany on August 23.

During the war, Japan gained German territory in China's Shantung Province, as well as Germany's island possessions in Micronesia. The Japanese navy checked the German fleet in the Pacific, and even provided protection for Allied merchant vessels in the Indian Ocean and the Mediterranean. Although Japan's role was limited, the war brought prosperity to Japanese industry by greatly stimulating both the civilian and military economies.

In the barely half a century following the Meiji Restoration, the small East Asian island nation had come a long way. Abandoning its policy of isolation, Japan had emerged victorious in its conflicts with China and Russia, and now stood alongside the Allied victors in the Great War. Its capitalist economy was also gaining momentum, so that in that sphere as well, Japan had to be counted among the Great Powers of Europe and America.

**

The last year of the Great War also brought important changes in Hirohito's life. On January 17, 1918, Princess Nagako, the fourteen-year-old daughter of Prince Kuni-yoshi Kuni, was chosen to be his bride. Hirohito was not involved in the selection of his prospective wife. Nagako was picked by senior members of the Imperial Household Ministry, and it would be another two years before he himself would be told about the choice. At the time of the unannounced betrothal, Hirohito was sixteen years old (not too young to get married in those days), but it would be several more years before the ceremony took place because both partners had to complete their respective "imperial educations."

Thus Princess Nagako embarked on her studies, in preparation for becoming the next empress of Japan. But barely six months later the engagement encountered unexpected difficulties. Somehow or other it was discovered that color blindness ran in Nagako's family. Her own eyes were fine, but there was a fear that if the trait were indeed hereditary in her family, the chances were fifty-fifty that it would be passed on to her children. It became a major issue in court circles, the flames being fanned by Aritomo Yamagata, a powerful holdover from the Meiji period. Yamagata demanded that Prince Kuni withdraw his daughter from the engagement. But the prince was a stubborn man. He delivered a threat to Prince Fushimi, his senior and an imperial messenger:

> It was the imperial house itself that asked for my daughter's hand. If the engagement is to be broken, it should be done by the imperial house. And I'd like to add that if that comes to pass, I shall be forced to answer the insult to me and my family by first stabbing Nagako to death, and then committing suicide myself.

The message was conveyed to Emperor Taishō, along with copies of medical reports showing that neither the prince nor Nagako suffered from color blindness. This in turn drew the anger of Prime Minister Takashi Hara*, who scolded, "This is surprisingly rude behavior, and not something the imperial family should be subjected to."

The opposition parties saw the issue as an opportunity to embarrass the government, and they lined up on Prince Kuni's side. Even right-wing thugs joined in, and the whole country was in an uproar. Of course, the government tried to keep the dispute out of the papers, but it spread by word of mouth, and even without the media became a major topic of discussion. The issue was further complicated because the disputants were split along regional lines as well. Yamagata represented the faction from Choshu Province, while Nagako's mother was from the rival Satsuma Province.

In the end it was decided that to break the engagement once it had been made would compromise the honor and integrity of the imperial house, so the betrothal was left to

*A list of the prime ministers of the Taishō and Shōwa periods is on page 210.

stand. But the whole incident showed just what kind of intrigue and machinations went on among royalty and the aristocracy, be it in the East or in the West.

***

As Hirohito neared the end of his seven years of special schooling, Prime Minister Hara began to consider sending him on a trip to Europe. Japan's standing in the world had risen dramatically, and as a result of the Great War its economy was getting stronger by the day. It seemed very important that the future Emperor Hirohito have a firsthand look at the advanced nations of the West and acquire a global perspective on the international scene. Furthermore, the fleet of warships by which he was to travel would serve to demonstrate imperial Japan's military power. In short, it would benefit both Hirohito and the nation, but Hara knew there were obstacles that threatened to prevent the trip.

First of all, there was Emperor Taishō's health. In an entry to his diary in November of 1919, Hara wrote:

> His Majesty suffered from meningitis as a child, and it has continued to affect his health adversely as he has gotten older. In particular, he often stutters when he reads aloud. On his last birthday address, he could barely deliver the simplest speech.

If the emperor were to die while Hirohito was abroad, there could be great confusion at home. Immediately upon the death of an emperor, there is supposed to be an accession ceremony for his heir, in which the new sovereign inherits the three imperial regalia—the sword, the jewel, and the mirror—as proof of his new position. In addition, there are a number of other ceremonies and rites to be performed. But if Hirohito were abroad, his return would take several weeks, which would delay these events and invite considerable trouble.

The second problem was that a sizable number of people opposed the trip. Some took an ethical stance: Was it not "unseemly" for the crown prince to leave the country while his father was ill? Others feared that the prince's safety could not be guaranteed while he was in foreign countries with lax protection. Their concern was not so much over Japanese nationals abroad but Korean terrorists, who had been a constant headache ever since Japan had annexed Korea in 1910. On top of all that, some suggested that Hirohito would be brainwashed by democracy. In those days democracy was labeled seditious by those who favored the imperial system. Ultranationalists and right-wingers, rallying behind one or more of these reasons, vowed to oppose the trip—with terrorist acts if necessary.

Hirohito's mother, the empress, ultraconservative by nature, was also against his traveling to Europe. Presumably she felt the same worries that any mother would about her son going off on a long trip to foreign lands. However, Hara persevered, patiently explaining the importance of the visit to the empress, until she finally understood what the trip would mean both to Hirohito and Japan, and gave her consent, albeit halfheartedly.

On March 3, 1921, Hirohito set out from Yokohama on the battleship *Katori*, escorted by a second warship, the *Kashima*. After Okinawa, all the ports of call along the way— Hong Kong, Singapore, Colombo, Aden, Suez, Port Said,

Malta, and Gibraltar—were British colonies, and because of the Anglo-Japanese Alliance, he received warm welcomes at each of them. Although these stops were all supposed to be unofficial, they were in fact treated as state visits by the British authorities, which laid on twenty-one-gun salutes and formal welcoming ceremonies. There could be no better indication of Japan's new status in the world than the welcome accorded to its crown prince by the British Empire.

On a more personal level, Hirohito's days at sea were far removed from his usual life as a "bird in a cage," as he himself described it. It is only a slight overstatement to say that the difference between the voyage and life in the palace was like the difference between heaven and hell for the crown prince.

On May 7, seventy-five days after leaving Yokohama, the two ships docked at Portsmouth in England. Edward, Prince of Wales, tall and just twenty-seven at the time, came out to meet the *Katori* when it anchored outside the harbor. As a military band played "God Save the King," he greeted Hirohito with a warm handshake. They boarded the royal train for the two-hour ride to London's Victoria Station. There they were met on the platform by King George V, the Duke of Connaught, and the Duke of York (later to ascend the throne as George VI after his brother's abdication).

Hirohito was a personal guest of the royal family for the next three days, and of the British government for a further five. From then until he left for France on May 29, Hirohito visited London and other parts of the British Isles. Wherever he went, he and his suite were treated with extreme kindness, and they were greatly affected by the warmth of their reception.

One day was particularly memorable. In addition to a large state dinner to which 128 guests were invited, King George arranged for Hirohito to enjoy an intimate family lunch at Buckingham Palace. Only royal family members were present, including the Duke of York and Queen Mary, and Japan's crown prince was treated like a member of the family himself. The conversation was relaxed and familiar. They spoke of Japan and its imperial family, and of Hirohito's experiences in the Mediterranean. Talk turned to the duties of a sovereign, and Hirohito left very impressed.

For the next three days, Hirohito and several members of his entourage stayed in rooms in the palace. During their stay King George bestowed upon Hirohito one of England's highest honors, the Order of the Bath, and also made him an honorary general in the British army. Tailors and a bootmaker were called to the palace to fit the young crown prince for his new military uniform, which was delivered several days later. Unlike the Japanese uniform with its stand-up collar, the British uniform was designed to be worn with a necktie, leather belt at the waist, and calf-length boots. Still considered a student in Japan, Hirohito normally wore a crew cut, but during the long voyage to England he had let his hair grow, and in his new uniform he looked every inch a general. In Japan his rank was still only major (in the army) or lieutenant-commander (in the navy), but all of a sudden he had been "promoted" five ranks. Thus clad, he formally reviewed the troops at Aldershot and inspected its barracks, military academy, and college.

Hirohito learned a great deal in England that he could not have learned in Japan. Above all, he developed a deep sense of gratitude and respect for the British royal family. These impressions stayed with him. Many years later after World War II, he remarked at a press conference, "For the rest of my life I shall never forget the fatherly warmth and wise counsel of His Majesty King George V."

On May 30, Hirohito reboarded the *Katori* at Portsmouth for the crossing to France. As the Japanese ships crossed the midway point in the English Channel, the British escort of nine warships turned back to England and were replaced by five destroyers flying the tricolor of France. Under a soft spring rain, they led the two Japanese ships into Le Havre.

As a high school student, Hirohito had studied French, and he was able to speak and read it with some fluency, so he felt rather comfortable and relaxed during his stay in France. It was just June, softly caressed by early summer breezes. As this was an unofficial visit, Hirohito and his entourage were able to sightsee at their leisure, climbing the Eiffel Tower, walking along the Champs-Elysées and strolling through the Bois de Boulogne.

One of the things Hirohito most wanted to do on his trip to Europe was to visit some of the World War I battlefields. As a student, the crown prince had been very fond of history, to the point where he had hoped to make it his field of specialization. But, discouraged by palace officials, who feared that an emperor who knew too much about Japan's history might be difficult to handle, he took up biology instead. Nevertheless, he had read with particular interest a book about the Great War and the toll it had taken in the short and long term. It made a deep impression on the young prince and contributed to his dislike of war. It also left him with a desire to visit some famous battlefields of that war and earlier conflicts.

Verdun, the Western Front, is 200 kilometers to the east of Paris. Hirohito's guide to this historic site was none other than Marshal Pétain, the veteran commander of the Verdun campaign. Five years had passed since the brutal seven-month battle, but the town of Verdun was still in ruins. Here and there stood blackened trees, and bullet-riddled metal helmets lay scattered about on the ground. Hirohito spent five hours touring the area by car. They drove past the notorious ''Bayonet Trench,'' in which several score French soldiers had been buried alive when a shell exploded nearby, just as they were about to charge. All that was left of them after the explosion were ten bayonet tips sticking out of the rubble.

Four days later Hirohito visited the Somme, where memorial crosses were lined up as far as the eye could see. There they caught sight of an old soldier leaning on a cane, walking slowly among the crosses, looking for the grave of a dead comrade. They also saw a war widow in her forties come out of a ruined house to sell postcards of the site. According to a member of his entourage, Hirohito was so moved by the eerie scene that he donated ten thousand francs for the victims of the Somme. His face drawn, the crown prince remarked, ''War is truly a cruel thing; anyone who admires war should come and see this place.'' And indeed, this tour of inspection served to confirm his dislike of war.

On September 3, 173 days after his departure, Hirohito

returned to Yokohama, having visited, in addition to Great Britain and France, three other European countries: Belgium, the Netherlands, and Italy.

Coming of Age

While Hirohito was away in Europe, Prime Minister Hara began to deliberate on what to do about Emperor Taishō. He had ascended the throne in 1912 at the age of thirty-three, but perhaps the responsibilities of government were too much for him, for the effects of his childhood illness seemed to become more pronounced year by year. Hara wrote in his diary: "Recently it has gotten to the point where one must do everything through the empress, and I am very concerned about the abuses this might lead to in the future."

Hara concluded that he had no choice but to ask Hirohito to serve as regent when he returned from his European trip. The regent acted in the name of the emperor if the latter became incapacitated and was unable to rule for some reason, and by imperial family precedent the position was the crown prince's if he was of age. However, there were several formidable obstacles that could prevent this from happening. First of all, since the emperor himself was not lucid enough to be fully aware of his condition, it was not clear whether on any given day he would consent to transferring his powers to a regent. Furthermore, his consort, Empress Sadako, was an intelligent, strong-willed woman who understood the uses of power. There was no guarantee that she would accept the arrangement either.

And then there was the privy council, which could handcuff the government in such matters. The council was the emperor's highest consulting body, and historically its councillors had proved to be the sitting cabinet's most troublesome adversaries. The appointment of a regent needed the approval of the Imperial Family Council as well. In addition to dealing with these two bodies, the government could hardly ignore public opinion. The general public was kept unaware of the emperor's health problems. As far as they knew, he was fine, and if he were suddenly forced to "retire," people would assume it was the result of some secret feud between the government and the palace, especially coming less than a year after the bitter dispute over Hirohito and Nagako's engagement.

In any case, Taishō's mental illness was worsening by the day, and there was no hope for his recovery. Something had to be done. Thanks to his perseverance and persuasive powers, Hara was able to obtain the agreement of the imperial family, the privy council, and the empress. The next step was to take his case to the people. On October 4 an announcement was made concerning the emperor's illness and its prognosis. Its detail and clarity left no doubts in people's minds, and the public accepted the situation.

Hara's plans were proceeding as he had hoped. He had decided on November 25, 1921, as the day to formally appoint Hirohito prince regent. But on November 4, the nation was shocked by the news that Hara had been assassinated by an eighteen-year-old ultranationalist. The murder threw the country into turmoil, but for Hirohito it was especially disheartening. Hara had been the one to arrange his trip to Europe in the face of severe domestic opposition, and Hirohito felt a debt of gratitude to him for it. It was one thing for Hara's opponents to be narrow-minded, but quite another for them to resort to terrorism, and Hirohito, indignant at this turn of events, was determined to go ahead with Hara's plans for him to be made regent. And in fact the naming did occur on November 25, as scheduled. For all practical purposes, Emperor Taishō's era was over, and Japan was entering the age of Hirohito.

* * *

On April 12, 1922, six months after Hirohito had become regent, Edward, Prince of Wales, came to Japan for a state visit. When Hirohito had visited England the year before, Edward and his father, King George V, had treated him with great hospitality, and he wanted to return the kindness.

Prince Edward was on a round-the-world trip aboard the cruiser *Renown*, escorted by a second warship, the *Durban*. Japan was his next port of call after the United States. Naturally he was treated as an official state guest. It had been a year since the two princes had last met. After a warm greeting such as Hirohito himself had received in England, Prince Edward was taken on a tour of Japan, traveling westward from Yokohama through Hakone, Kyoto, and Nara, and finally on to Kagoshima, where he reboarded the

Renown to continue his journey. Wherever he went, Prince Edward's unconventional yet refined nature caused a stir among the Japanese. Hirohito may have envied those qualities of easy dignity and sociability, which he himself lacked, but he could not change his nature, and besides, such attributes were not deemed appropriate to a Japanese sovereign in those days. On the contrary, the Imperial Household Ministry did everything it could to discourage him from showing any kind of populist tendencies.

For his part, Hirohito, having looked at other monarchies in the world, wanted to bring about a fundamental, enlightened change in the Japanese imperial system. He wanted to demystify the throne, eliminate some of its authoritarian aspects, and give it a more democratic character. Beyond that, he wanted to encourage contact with the people, something that had always been unimaginable. Unfortunately these plans were quickly forestalled.

Hirohito made his first move toward change when he returned from his trip to Europe. He decided to throw a homecoming party for himself at the Akasaka Detached Palace and invite his school friends. He began the festivities by announcing, "For the next two hours, please forget that I am crown prince. Let us not stand on ceremony."

His young companions let out a cheer and started the celebration. Just as they had been told, they relaxed and were soon behaving in a most familiar manner toward Hirohito. The stiff palace chamberlains were appalled at such goings-on and stood by, scowling. They later told the lord keeper of the privy seal all about the party, and it eventually came to the attention of Prince Saionji. The prince was from the highest ranks of the nobility, had twice served as prime minister late in the Meiji period, and even now was considered an elder statesman of great influence. He admonished the crown prince sternly, warning him that such antics undermined the very foundations of the throne and threatened its dignity and absolute authority. He considered it a grave matter indeed. Though crown prince and regent, Hirohito was still only twenty years old. Moreover, he was introverted and not especially forceful. Unable to stand up to Saionji, who was lecturing him like a teacher, he could only listen.

Still, it is unfortunate that Hirohito's first faltering attempt to bring some fresh air into the palace was so pitifully crushed, for it left him thereafter too timid to attempt any other similar reforms.

* * *

After Hirohito turned twenty-one on April 29, 1922, the Imperial Household Ministry began making plans to set a date for his wedding. On his twenty-first birthday, Hirohito and his intended, Princess Nagako, met again after a long separation. She was brought to the palace for the meeting, but they were only allowed to talk for a few moments. Not quite two months later, on June 20, the match received imperial sanction, and the impending marriage was publicly announced. Five and half years had passed since the engagement had been quietly decided upon, and Princess Nagako was now nineteen years old—a little on the late side for marriage, some said. The main reason for the long delay was probably Yamagata's opposition to the marriage. But on February 1, 1922, Aritomo Yamagata died at the age of eighty-four, and the pall he had cast over palace life was lifted. At last, on April 12, 1923, the Imperial Household Ministry announced that the imperial wedding would take place in the latter part of November that same year. Prince Kuni and his daughter could relax and begin their preparations.

But another obstacle arose: the Great Kanto Earthquake and Fire, which left Tokyo, Yokohama, and the surrounding areas in ruins. The quake, measuring 7.9 on the Richter scale, struck on September 1, 1923. The damage was unprecedented. The loss in human life alone was staggering: 140,000. Three quarters of the Tokyo-Yokohama megalopolis—the heart of the modern Japanese nation—was completely destroyed.

Princess Nagako was now almost twenty. Prince Kuni was becoming irritated by the repeated delays in the wedding plans. Forceful by nature, he insisted that the marriage take place as soon as possible, and would not back down. He worried that with each postponement another obstacle seemed to arise. The wedding was set for January 26, 1924. And so, on that day, Hirohito and Nagako were at last married in the imperial palace sanctuary in Tokyo, a full six years after their engagement. Although the ceremony was completed and the couple officially joined, the public reception was postponed until May 31 (it lasted five days more) because Tokyo had not yet recovered from the earthquake and fire. The couple's honeymoon, too, was put off until August. From August 3 the couple did spend a month traveling. They first went to Nikko, then on to Fukushima Prefecture, where they stayed at Okinajima on Lake Inawashiro.

One of the first things Hirohito did for his new wife was

to reorganize the palace ladies-in-waiting. The old system with its numerous ranks was stifling and promoted intrigue and rivalry. It also gave the ladies enormous power over the daily lives of those who lived in the palace. The ladies were required to speak a special form of Japanese exclusive to the court. Furthermore, they were all drawn from the ranks of the aristocracy. Hirohito opened the doors. He abolished the various ranks, so that all ladies-in-waiting were now equal, and he allowed commoners to serve as well. He also encouraged the use of standard Japanese in the palace. In this way, he ensured that he and Nagako, emperor and empress, husband and wife, would truly run their own household, and in a sense this was his most important wedding gift to his new bride.

The newlyweds moved into the Akasaka Detached Palace. Hirohito went once or twice a week to the main palace, but most of his official duties could be carried out at the Akasaka residence, so he had plenty of time to spend getting to know his new wife. Nagako, who loved music, would play the piano for her husband or sing for him in a soprano voice. Or she might invite him to listen to records with her.

To the south of the palace was a large garden planted with trees and plants of the four seasons, so that each in turn would flower or change color. The prince regent would take his wife for a stroll there, and as they walked along he would show his considerable knowledge of botany by naming the various trees and describing the process by which the flowers bloomed.

Biology lab facilities were soon set up inside the Akasaka Detached Palace compound, and the prince regent was able to start pursuing his research in earnest. In addition to a

1,620-square-foot lab, there was a shed for raising animals and a half-acre field for growing plants. Professor Hattori, Hirohito's old biology tutor, was called in to oversee the facilities.

***

On December 6, 1925, with the whole nation waiting and watching, Nagako gave birth to a daughter. The first princess, who was ten days overdue, weighed about 3,300 grams (roughly seven and a quarter pounds) at birth. She was an attractive baby with large, bright eyes. On the seventh night after her birth, she was given the name Princess Teru Shigeko.

As if to dash cold water on the joy surrounding the birth of an imperial princess, Emperor Taishō's illness was growing worse. About ten days after Princess Teru was born, the emperor collapsed in the bathroom. A chamberlain waiting in the next room heard the noise through the partition and rushed in to find the emperor lying on the floor moaning. He was left where he was while the palace doctor was summoned. The doctor decided it was not the heart attack they had feared but a mild stroke. After giving the emperor first aid, they moved him to his sleeping quarters.

However, his condition continued to deteriorate rapidly, and he had another attack. His speech was now impaired, and he became unable to walk. In addition, his memory and powers of discrimination were fading. In August he was moved to Hayama, but he only continued to weaken day by day, and in December he contracted pneumonia. The ministrations of his wife and the court doctors proved in vain, and at 1:25 A.M. on December 25, 1926, he passed away at the age of forty-seven.

A few hours before he died, an unseasonable rainstorm had struck the Hayama area, and twice peals of thunder had echoed across the landscape. The heavy rains pounding the roof tiles of the Hayama Detached Palace inspired in those inside, already sunk in sorrow, an even deeper sense of foreboding.

Emperor Taishō has been called "the tragic emperor." Soon after his birth he contracted meningitis, which was to affect his health in later life. As a child, he was rather sickly but had a sunny disposition. When his family was staying at Numazu or Hayama, he would slip out of the house and wander around town. On these excursions he would often visit the Uematsu family, which lived in an old farm house several kilometers west of the Numazu Detached Palace. The young prince would enter the sitting room and just make himself at home. The Uematsus understood, and whenever they saw him coming they would prepare tea and cakes and take care of him.

As he grew to adulthood his restless nature became more and more evident. When his elder advisers or the prime minister came to the palace, he would grab a handful of cigarettes from the table and say, "Thanks for all your efforts. Now, here, have a smoke!" When the mood hit him, he would sing military songs, or recite poetry. And before his final illness he used to take great pleasure in having the imperial guards amuse him by assembling in the garden in front of the palace to perform martial music, play tug-of-war, or engage in comic dialogs or other such diversions.

Surely if he had not been shackled by the constraints imposed on him by the title "emperor," he might have enjoyed a longer, happier life. He must have hated being compared to Emperor Meiji, who was larger than life, and must have resented, too, the way his strong-willed wife kept him in check. The story—and a rather sad one it is, too—goes that he would sneak into the pantry and enjoy a cup of saké, admonishing the servants to "keep it secret from my wife."

He was on the throne for barely fifteen years, and ironically his main accomplishment (although it seems strange to call it that) was that he fathered four sons, thus ensuring the continuation of the main imperial line. The previous two emperors, Kōmei and Meiji, had each had only one son. If the sickly Emperor Taishō had not had a son, the throne would have been in a precarious state. In those days there were twelve princely houses with equal claims to the succession if the main line failed to produce an heir.

***

On the night of Emperor Taishō's death, Hirohito performed the *Kenji Togyo,* the ritual confirming his accession as Japan's 124th emperor, in the Hayama Detached Palace. During the short ceremony, the new emperor was entrusted with two of the imperial regalia, the sword and the jewel—objects of great antiquity, believed to have been given to the first Japanese emperor by the sun goddess—and with two seals, the imperial seal and the seal of state. At the same moment, in the imperial sanctuary in Tokyo, a Shinto priest reported the accession to the gods. This called for a separate ceremony because the third part of the imperial regalia, the sacred mirror, cannot be moved from the palace sanctuary.

Meanwhile, in the new villa buildings some 200 meters east of the annex where the deceased emperor's remains lay, the privy council convened in an emergency session, and chose "Shōwa" ("Illustrious Harmony") as the name of the era that was about to begin. By custom, era names like imperial names are chosen from passages in the ancient Chinese classics. "Shōwa" came from a section of the *Shu Ching* (*The Scripture of Documents*): "The hundred clans are *illustrious*; the ten thousand nations are in *harmony*."

When Hirohito took possession of the imperial regalia, the reign of the Taishō Emperor officially ended and the Shōwa era began. Hirohito's formal coronation took place on November 10, 1928, at the Kyoto Imperial Palace, the scene of imperial ceremonies for more than one thousand years. Each of the two ceremonies, accession and coronation, has its own significance. The accession marks the crown prince's assumption of the position of emperor, while the coronation amounts to a formal announcement of this to the world at large, and is Japan's most important public ceremony. Until the reign of Emperor Meiji (reigned 1868–1912), these had been very simple affairs, but due to Japan's increasing world prominence and growing nationalism at home, the Shōwa coronation turned into a magnificent, dazzling spectacle unparalleled in Japanese history.

All of Japan's leaders participated in the grand event, from the opening ceremonies on the tenth through the eight days of celebrations and banquets that followed. The coronation banquet lasted throughout the day and into the night, and was attended by 4,000 guests, a scale difficult to imagine, especially considering the historical circumstances.

The world was still suffering from the recession that had followed World War I. Japan had not fully recovered from the Great Kanto Earthquake of 1923, and worse yet, signs of financial panic had been evident since the spring of the previous year. A number of banks had been forced to close, small and medium-sized businesses were going bankrupt, and the unemployment rate was rising dramatically. As the economic crisis worsened, it would not have been surprising had the celebrations been the object of public contempt and resentment as they became more and more extravagant. But this did not happen. The Japanese, full of reverence for the imperial house, and fascinated by a ceremony that seemed like a beautiful painting displayed before their eyes, responded with joy and congratulations.

PART TWO:

THE EMPEROR AT WAR

The Limits of Power

The first half of the Shōwa era was marked by the struggle between an emperor who wanted peace and a military that was running out of control. As commander in chief, the emperor directed the army, and for their part, servicemen were expected to "take absolute loyalty as their primary duty," according to Emperor Meiji's *Imperial Rescript to Soldiers and Sailors*. However, the earliest indication that this ideal was breaking down came with the assassination of the Manchurian warlord Chang Tso-lin in 1928.

The pro-Japanese Chang took Peking in 1927, thus securing control over all of northern China. But from the south, Chiang Kai-shek's Kuomintang forces, hoping to unify all of China, launched a full-scale assault on the north in April 1928, forcing Chang's troops back. At that point the Japanese government became concerned that Japanese residing in Shantung Province might get caught in the crossfire. In Nanking and Hankow there had already been incidents in which Japanese had been murdered, raped, and robbed by Chinese nationals.

The emperor made his opposition to any Japanese military intervention clear: "A rash military expedition would antagonize the Chinese, and might well result in a replay of the Nikolaevsk Incident." (In 1920, Russian partisans had massacred a Japanese expeditionary force at Nikolaevsk in Siberia.)

But Prime Minister General Giichi Tanaka, already deeply enmeshed in his plans for China, proceeded to send the Kumamoto Division to the continent. In May, Japanese and Chinese Nationalist troops faced each other at Jinan in Shantung Province. When soldiers from the Chinese side attacked a Japanese business, the two armies engaged, with the Japanese scoring a victory.

One month later, Chang Tso-lin, who had been forced out of Peking by Chiang's troops, was returning to his Manchurian base in Mukden when the train on which he was riding was blown up, killing all on board. Since the incident occurred on the Manchurian Railroad, on land leased by Japan, the Japanese were quick to react. Their investigation concluded that "the incident was the work of plain-clothed soldiers from the south (part of Chiang Kai-shek's terrorist organization)." This was no more than an attempt to cover up the truth, for in fact the whole thing had been planned by Colonel Kōmoto, a senior staff officer in the Kwantung Army, part of Japan's forces in Manchuria.

At that time Manchuria was known as "Japan's lifeline." Japan felt it had earned special rights to the region, having spilled the blood of over 100,000 men in the Sino-Japanese and Russo-Japanese wars. Chang had been governing Manchuria with Japanese backing, but he had begun showing signs of independence, even rebellion.

However, more than anything else, Chang was killed because of Japan's ambition to assert direct control over the area.

The truth about the incident slowly began to leak out. Not only from China but from various European countries as well came expressions of doubt and skepticism about Japan's version of the story. The opposition parties, ready to make the matter a political issue, commenced attacking the government in the Diet. The Kwantung Army, fearing a loss of prestige, stuck to its story, leaving the Tanaka cabinet faced with a serious dilemma.

The emperor, too, was deeply troubled. He hinted that the punishment of those responsible would satisfactorily resolve the matter, but the prime minister, unable to control the military, simply tried to play down the situation, saying: "There is no proof that the offenders were members of the Kwantung Army, but I will carry out a full investigation, and if there is any fault on our side, I shall deal with the matter sternly."

Such equivocation irritated Hirohito, who made his displeasure evident by saying: "No matter what sort of man Chang Tso-lin may have been, he was the designated authority in Manchuria. It was very wrong of the Army to have any hand in his assassination." A chastened Prime Minister Tanaka ordered War Minister Yoshinori Shirakawa to come up with a secret report for the emperor.

With secret reports of this nature, it was customary to solicit the emperor's opinion privately before formally filing the document. The report read in part: "The army was not involved, but since this affair occurred in an overseas possession, those responsible for security have been punished." It went on to describe the light punishments meted out to Colonel Kōmoto and two other officers.

As the emperor looked the document over, his face hardened, and he said harshly, "Does this not contradict what you told me before?"

The war minister, embarrassed, started to make excuses. "I could offer a number of explanations for that. . ."

But the emperor cut him off, saying, "I have no need to hear your explanations." He then left the room.

Visibly upset, he confided to Grand Chamberlain Admiral Kantarō Suzuki: "I don't understand the prime minister or war minister at all. I don't want to listen to them anymore." He was apparently quite angry at the way they had deceived him and had disregarded his opinions. Prime Minister Tanaka resigned immediately. However, at the last cabinet meeting convened to secure the letters of resignation of cabinet members, one minister took a very hard line: "To treat the nation's prime minister so lightly, even once, is a serious matter. It would have been proper to remonstrate with His Majesty over this." The whole thing created quite a stir.

After the war the emperor himself recalled how he had overstepped constitutional bounds in this case, but said in his defense, "I was too young at the time." And indeed, it seems that among the emperor's close associates in those days it was often whispered about that the emperor was, after all, human, and prone to the errors of youth.

Had Hirohito gone too far by forcing the cabinet to resign, as he himself believed? Although the Meiji Constitution defined the emperor as an absolute sovereign, it also bound him to follow the advice of the prime minister in all matters of government. This arrangement had worked well during the reigns of the emperors Meiji and Taishō because their advisers, the men who had created the Meiji state and written its constitution, exercised the imperial prerogative. Their passing (Aritomo Yamagata, the last of Emperor Meiji's advisers, had died in 1922), deprived the state of any central unifying authority. During the 1920s the political parties, led by men such as Takashi Hara and Tsuyoshi Inukai, had almost succeeded in replacing the emperor's extra-constitutional advisers and establishing a parliamentary form of government on the British model. But by late 1920s the tide was turning against democracy. The military and their allies in the bureaucracy sought to manipulate the emperor's enormous powers for their own ends.

***

The Chang Tso-lin incident showed the emperor's hard side, but he had a softer, weaker side as well. An entry in a diary kept by one of his military attachés notes: "Saionji severely criticized Hirohito's lack of courage." Saionji, acting as a kind of tutor, accompanied Hirohito on his trip to Europe. His frank, hot-blooded personality contrasted with the emperor's own gentle, deliberate nature, and he must have found something lacking in Hirohito.

In another instance Hirohito's father-in-law, Prince Kuni, just one hour before his death, awoke suddenly from a coma and cried out, "I wish to speak to the empress." He told his daughter: "The reigning emperor is rather weak-willed at times. Therefore, he will need your support. Be strong! Be strong!" These were his last words.

But these criticisms of a young emperor changed to cries of admiration at the great coronation parade held on December 15, 1928. Seventy-four thousand students and young people from Tokyo and surrounding areas massed on the large plaza in front of the palace for the event. It was a bitterly cold day, with a chill December rain falling. The participants, all lined up for the parade, turned up the collars of their overcoats, rubbing their hands. At the head of the grounds a throne had been set out underneath a tent decorated with the imperial crest, but as the time for the parade drew near, workmen appeared and noisily dismantled the tent. A stir arose in the crowd as people wondered whether they were going to cancel the event. Some even seemed relieved. But a messenger appeared and announced in a loud voice: "The emperor sympathizes with the young people here being pelted by the rain and has ordered the tent taken down. He will review the parade from 2:00 as planned." This moved the students deeply. One of them removed his overcoat and laid it on the ground, and immediately everyone followed suit.

At the appointed time, the emperor arrived, and as he stepped out of the car the chamberlain threw an army cape over his shoulders. But when Hirohito climbed the reviewing stand, looked out over the plaza, and saw all the young people without their coats, he immediately unbuttoned his own and removed it. To the seventy-four thousand pairs of eyes fixed upon him, it was a solemn, dramatic moment. The ministers in attendance followed the emperor's lead.

The parade began. Burning with emotion, paying no mind to the rain, the youngsters marched, troop after troop, with firm step past the emperor, who for his part stood stock-still for an hour and twenty minutes, acknowledging each passing group with a salute, not once wavering. In the end, that inauspicious rain actually strengthened the bond between the emperor and his young subjects.

***

In October 1929 the world was plunged into financial panic by the collapse of the New York stock market. This in turn aggravated the chronic recession that had plagued the Japanese economy since the end of the Great War. "I have a college degree, but . . ." ran the lines of a popular song lamenting the bleak unemployment situation. On one side, there was the growing social problem of desperate farming families selling their daughters into prostitution. In contrast, scandals continually rocked the country as, in the words of another song, popular among rightists, "the rulers flaunt their position, the big companies boast of their wealth."

These desperate circumstances created a powder keg— one which exploded on September 18, 1931, with the Manchurian Incident. On that day, at Lake Lukochiao in the vicinity of Mukden, a bomb exploded, destroying the tracks of the South Manchurian Railway, which was run by a Japanese government-sponsored company. Blaming the act on Chinese forces, the Kwantung Army proceeded at once to attack the Chinese garrison at Mukden and occupy the whole of Manchuria.

In fact, after Chang Tso-lin's assassination, his son, Chang Hsüeh-liang had been trying to stir up anti-Japanese sentiment throughout Manchuria. Several staff officers of the Kwantung Army hoped to get rid of Chang, establish a new government in the region, and prepare to face the Soviet threat they saw there. Colonel Itagaki, Lieutenant-Colonel Ishiwara and Colonel Doihara, the head of intelligence operations in Mukden (Itagaki and Doihara were executed as Class "A" war criminals after the war), skirted the normal channels of the central command and came up with the scheme to stage the bombing. The three were determined to drag the army into the incident, for once the troops were committed, their plan for the conquest of Manchuria would be well on its way to realization. The emperor was deeply concerned and repeatedly called on the war minister and the army chief of staff not to let the situation get out of hand. But the army, for reasons of its own, pressed ahead.

In 1922, Japan had joined Europe, Canada, and the United States in signing the Nine-Power Pact, respecting China's territorial integrity, and in 1928 had signed the Kellogg-Briand Pact, renouncing war as a means of resolving disputes. All this the army swept away with one violent gesture.

Hirohito's military attaché was about to enter the emperor's chambers one day during this period, when he heard a sad soliloquy from beyond the door: "Again, again . . . They're at it again. Once again, the army has gone and done something stupid, and this is the result! Wouldn't it be simpler just to give Manchuria back to Chang Hsüeh-liang?" The aide was left with a vivid image of his troubled sovereign, alone in his room, pacing back and forth, muttering to himself. Indeed, it was the emperor's habit to wander up and down the room, talking to himself, when he was troubled or upset about something.

By January 1932 the flames of war in China had reached as far as Shanghai. Incidents such as the kidnapping of five Japanese Buddhist priests by Chinese troops and the trading of fire between naval forces gave the army a perfect excuse to dispatch its troops.

Mamoru Shigemitsu of Japan's China legation kept the emperor up-to-date with the negotiations with the Nationalist government, and Hirohito was disappointed at how unbending everyone was. "For now it seems that goodwill between Japan and China is impossible," he lamented.

Staffers in the expeditionary force, spurred on by their victories, wanted to capture the Nationalists' capital, Nanking, and were not about to stop, but General Yoshinori Shirakawa, obedient to the imperial will, held them in check and proclaimed a cease-fire on March 3, 1932. At this juncture an agreement was reached with the Chinese, and troops were withdrawn. Unfortunately, shortly thereafter General Shirakawa was wounded by a hand grenade thrown by a Korean terrorist at a party celebrating the emperor's birthday in Shanghai. He died of his injuries one month later. After the general's death, Hirohito's wishes for a prompt cessation of hostilities became stronger than ever. Of course, he was concerned about the reaction of the League of Nations, which planned to meet in early March to discuss the Manchurian situation and was almost certain to be critical of Japan.

Shirakawa's death was treated as a casualty of war, and his name was added to the honor roll at Yasukuni, a Shinto shrine in Tokyo dedicated to the souls of those who die in battle. At Yasukuni's annual festival the following spring, Hirohito bowed before the shrine and secretly shed tears for the loyalty of the late general who alone in the army understood and sought to obey the emperor's will. Using the timely imagery of the annual spring Doll Festival (for on that day one year earlier General Shirakawa had declared the cease-fire), the emperor expressed his deepest emotions in a poem that he sent to the general's widow:

> Well I recall how bravely
> He brought an end to the fighting
> On that very day
> When Heavenly Maidens celebrate
> The Festival of Dolls

Hirohito's action was unorthodox, and out of fear that it might antagonize the military, the poem was kept secret. He had praised Shirakawa's bravery in *avoiding* war, not *waging* it. And he seemed also to be lamenting the fact that so few of his other generals had Shirakawa's backbone.

***

The general public, unaware of the emperor's desire for peace, unanimously backed the military and rejoiced that Manchuria had been returned to Japanese control. The striking victories of the ''Emperor's Army'' fed the people's pride and ignited their enthusiasm. Moreover, the military, for its part, was cunning enough to keep pushing the emperor out front, claiming that everything was being done in his name. Thus, his ''loyal subjects'' believed that dominion over China was all in accordance with the imperial will.

In March 1932, six months after subduing the greater part of Manchuria, Japan established the puppet state of Manchukuo with the deposed Chinese emperor Pu Yi as head of state. Faced with Japan's obvious long-term plans for territorial expansion, the League of Nations dispatched a commission headed by Lord Lytton to investigate the situation. As expected, the commission's report was harsh, rejecting Japan's claim that it had acted in self-defense. Furthermore, the report noted, the establishment of Manchukuo had not been a spontaneous local movement: The regime was opposed by most of the local people.

The army called for Japan's immediate withdrawal from the League of Nations, and the hawks argued irrationally that as Japanese troops had already advanced as far as the Mongolian Province of Jehol on the northern borders of China, they should proceed without delay to occupy Peking and Tientsin.

Two or three times the emperor had called on his chiefs of staff, the prime minister, and the war minister to halt the Jehol campaign, but those in the field came up with one excuse after an other. Nara, the emperor's chief military attaché, recorded in his diary: "His Majesty is suspicious of the Army. I had hoped the troops in the field would desist in accordance with the high command's orders. His Majesty was in a bad mood. . . . He was rather worked up."

When the Lytton Commission report was debated at the League in February 1933, Japan suffered a disastrous defeat: The General Assembly voted 42 to 1 (Japan casting the dissenting vote) to condemn Japan's actions in Manchuria. Only Siam (Thailand) abstained. Japan's representative, Yōsuke Matsuoka, kicked his chair in disgust and walked out. Japan withdrew from the League and readied itself to face its future as an outsider in the international community. As the government prepared its formal announcement of withdrawal, the emperor suggested adding the following two points:

(1) It is truly regrettable that we have reached the point where we must withdraw.

(2) Even after withdrawal, we will strive to preserve international friendship and harmony.

The new "nation" of Manchukuo was decorated throughout with slogans written by Colonel Itagaki and Lieutenant-Colonel Ishiwara such as "The Five Peoples in Harmony" and "A Joyous Land Under the Monarchy," and the Japanese there enthusiastically went about trying to build their ideal new society. But in fact, among the "Five Peoples," only the Japanese counted, and they dominated the other four: the Manchurians, Chinese, Mongolians, and Koreans. It was a nation that served to bolster the self-importance of the Japanese army.

Pu Yi did not actually ascend the Manchukuo throne until 1934, and since he and his consort had no children, it was assumed that his successor would be his younger brother, Pu Jie. A marriage was arranged between a daughter of the Marquis Saga and Pu Jie, just as earlier, when Japan had annexed Korea, the Japanese arranged a match between a Japanese princess and Korea's crown prince.

In 1935, Pu Yi was brought to Japan on the battleship *Hie* for a state visit. Hirohito greeted him warmly at Tokyo

Station, and the two emperors exchanged firm handshakes. This was the first time in Japanese history that a head of state had visited Japan, and the moment was captured on film. In those days, it was not unusual for newspapers to run posed photographs of the emperor at formal receptions, but this picture, not made public until after the war, showed a close-up of Hirohito's smiling face as he stood on the platform, waiting for the train to pull in.

Until after the war the Imperial Household Ministry subjected photographs of the emperor to the strictest censorship. To the despair of photographers, they would often prohibit any picture that they considered unflattering. Another photograph that did not see the light of day until after the war was one taken in 1936 of the whole imperial family at the Hayama Detached Palace. It showed the emperor dressed in a suit, standing with the rest of his family. It presents an altogether charming scene but was suppressed. The reason given—odd as it may seem—that it compromised the dignity of the "god among mortals," as the emperor was then described. Indeed, even the photographs that showed the emperor smiling were censored.

Shortly after the establishment of Manchukuo, Pu Yi quickly found reason to feel disenchantment with his "ally" Japan. Perhaps part of it was that he realized he was nothing but a puppet of the Kwantung Army, but the main problem was the heavy-handed way the Japanese treated him. To the world, Pu Yi was presented as the ruler of Manchukuo, but the reality presented a very different and much darker picture. Pu Yi's actions—even his basic human rights—were restricted, and although he sat on the emperor's throne, it must have felt more like a bed of nails.

This was made especially clear to him the first time he visited Japan. His younger brother and sister, as well as his brother-in-law, were all in Japan at the time, but none was allowed to meet him, not even at Tokyo Station. Pu Yi may have been emperor of Manchukuo, but as far as the Japanese were concerned, his siblings were just ordinary citizens.

At the request of the Manchurian ambassador, who was appalled at the slight, the three relatives were finally permitted to meet Pu Yi at the Akasaka Palace Guest House, but even then it was for only five minutes! They barely had time to exchange greetings before being ushered out. Prince Chichibu heard about the incident and felt sorry for all concerned. He arranged to have the siblings invited to a function for Pu Yi, and the family members were at last able to meet and talk at their leisure.

In the end, while Empress Nagako seemed to enjoy Pu Yi's company immensely, Hirohito had a much lower opinion of him, and in general Pu Yi's dealings with the Japanese did not seem to be very pleasant. It is perhaps not surprising, then, that after the war, in his writing and at the Tokyo War Crimes Tribunal, Pu Yi was so vitriolic in his criticisms of Hirohito and Japan.

Patriots and Soldiers

Japan's military successes overseas did not improve matters at home. The political situation was deteriorating rapidly, and the farmers were beset by a combination of bad harvests and low agricultural prices. This spurred a group of young officers and radical rightists, "burning with moral indignation," into acts of terrorism with the avowed goal of bringing about a "national reorganization." In March and in October 1931, radical officers backed by senior army leaders plotted to overthrow the government. On both occasions the coups were aborted at the last moment, and the plotters were let off with token punishments. In the spring of the following year, after the assassination in February of former finance minister Junnosuke Inoue by members of the the ultranationalistic Ketsumeidan (Blood League) secret society, a band of commissioned navy officers and army cadets attacked and murdered Prime Minister Tsuyoshi Inukai in his official residence in what is known as the May 15 Incident. Inukai was an honest politician, untainted by scandal, but the young officers' goal was to bring down party government, so they closed their eyes and went on a rampage. The public viewed the perpetrators as heroes and called for leniency in their punishment.

After the May 15 Incident, the emperor was determined to do what he could to save the situation, both domestically and overseas. In a highly unusual move, Hirohito dispatched Grand Chamberlain Suzuki to Prince Saionji's residence to convey the qualifications he was looking for in the late Prime Minister Inukai's successor. Saionji, as the only surviving and least powerful of Emperor Meiji's advisers, was the one to recommend a new prime minister. The emperor made the following points:

(1) That the new prime minister should be someone of excellent character;

(2) That cleaning up the political scene and strictly enforcing military discipline in the army and the navy would depend above all on the strength of character of the new prime minister;

(3) That anyone with fascist leanings was out of the question;

(4) That the new prime minister must uphold the constitution, for not to do so was an offense to Emperor Meiji; and

(5) That in foreign affairs peace should be the fundamental principle, and harmonious international relations should be sought.

Hirohito added further remarks directed at the war minister: "Recently it seems that young people have been going a little too far. At such times the minister should be prepared to sacrifice everything in order to bring the situation under control.'' Even this rather broad hint directed at the military fell on deaf ears, as they only grew more and more arrogant.

***

In the early 1900s, Dr. Tatsukichi Minobe, a leading authority on constitutional law and a professor at the University of Tokyo, propounded the theory of the emperor as an organ of the state in a book entitled *An Outline of the Constitution*. This ''emperor theory,'' influenced by the works of the German legal theorist Georg Jellinek, gained wide acceptance in intellectual circles. It held that the state was a kind of corporate entity and that such aspects as justice or the authority of the ruler were organs of that corporate state. The emperor exercised his executive functions as the highest of these organs.

Minobe's theory, which conflicted with the view that the emperor was an absolute sovereign, was strongly opposed by the militarists and rightists. From the standpoint of the military, it was much better to have a strong emperor, and the rightists, who virtually worshipped the emperor, could never accept the idea that he was an organ of the state.

But Minobe's work had become firmly established in the academic community after his debates over the Meiji Constitution with the leading conservative thinkers who saw the emperor as absolute. When Minobe first propounded his theory, the issue of disrespect toward the emperor did not arise at all, nor did anyone accuse him of the offense of lèse-majesté. But as society drifted toward the right, Minobe's ideas became increasingly controversial. The one to launch an all-out attack on Minobe was Baron Takeo Kikuchi, a retired lieutenant-general in the army, and, like Minobe, a member of the House of Peers.

Proud of his bloodline—his family had served the imperial house since the fourteenth century—Kikuchi delivered, in 1935, a blistering attack on Minobe that put a great deal of pressure on the government, and touched off a clamorous war of words in both houses of the Diet. The gist of Kikuchi's denunciation was: "To regard the sacred Emperor as an 'organ' of the state is the height of disrespect, and amounts to treason. Can we just let this sort of thing go on?"

War Minister Senjūrō Hayashi added, "As far as I am concerned, it would be most distressing if a theory like this were allowed to stir up the masses. I believe such doctrines should be stamped out."

When Dr. Minobe tried rational argument to defend the theory in the Diet, he was shouted down for an entire hour. Not only the right wing and the military but even veterans' groups united to form a powerful lobby calling for the suppression of the theory. The Diet unanimously passed a resolution calling for a clarification of the national polity. Kisaburō Suzuki, head of the ruling Seiyūkai party, rubbed salt on the wounds. Claiming that "there is a state because there is a emperor, not an emperor because there is a state," he demanded sanctions against Minobe's theory as well as his books. Minobe was even branded an "academic outlaw."

Minobe refused to recant and insisted on the correctness of his theory, knowing that emotional arguments could not undermine a scholarly legal principle. Eventually, however, the government banned three of his books, and he was warned that since he refused to recant, if he did not resign from the House of Peers, charges would be brought against him. As worried for his friends as for himself, Minobe felt compelled to resign. Even so, sometime later a rightist attacked him at his home and left him seriously injured.

What did Hirohito think of this theory that saw him as an organ of state? It appears that Grand Chamberlain Suzuki once confidentially relayed to Baron Harada the emperor's feelings on the matter. He quoted Hirohito as saying:

> When it comes to the larger debate over whether sovereignty lies with the ruler or with the state, this emotional argument over whether the organ theory is good or bad is really quite foolish. I myself am inclined to believe in the sovereignty of the state over that of the ruler, mainly because the latter view can all too easily lead to despotism. In a country like Japan, where ruler and nation are one and the same, what is wrong with the organ theory?
>
> Many people are criticizing Minobe these days, but there is nothing disloyal about him. Is there anyone else of his stature these days? It is sad, indeed, that such a fine scholar should be treated in this manner.

World history gives us many examples of rulers who sought to expand their power, but very few have approved of limiting their own authority.

Hirohito's interest in the Minobe affair almost became an obsession. Once when he read a news report that suggested that Minobe was about to be indicted, he immediately had the justice minister find out if it was true. When the emperor learned that the article had been pure speculation, he showed great displeasure, saying, "The government should have some control over such false reports." It was a time when newspapers were being subjected to censorship, and it gives us an idea how worried Hirohito was about Minobe.

As a result of this fruitless debate, which dragged on for a full year, the professor himself was forced to resign both from his academic position as well as his seat in the House of Peers. Ironically, the Seiyūkai party, which had formed a political organization to attack Minobe's theories, was defeated in the 1936 elections by the Minseitō party, in one of the biggest upsets in Japanese political history. Kisaburō Suzuki, who had been one of Minobe's most outspoken critics, lost the election for the leadership of the Seiyūkai party.

* * *

The winter of 1936 was snowier than usual, especially in the early hours of February 26, when a great deal of snow fell in Tokyo before sunrise. As the sun rose over a landscape pure white as far as the eye could see, it rose on a day that would see the first attempted coup d'état in Japanese history.

Beginning with the Ketsumeidan activities and the May 15 Incident, increasing unrest among radical young military officers and extreme right-wing groups was sending out ominous signals, but the government was floundering in its own incompetence, and it seemed that the political parties and *zaibatsu* (business cartels) were doing their best to live up to their portrayal by right-wingers, who accused them of collusion and single-mindedly pursuing their own interests.

Among the general population, resentment over the way politicians were handling the worsening economic crisis was ready to boil over. This, coupled with the fact that the overseas situation in Manchuria and China was heating up, led many to feel that Japan needed a "Shōwa Restoration," that is, a national reorganization as revolutionary as the Meiji Restoration, with a kind of totalitarian form of government as its goal.

Most of the discontented young officers were attached to the First Army Division in Tokyo. The high command, worried about their explosive potential, announced that the division would be sent to Manchuria, effective April 1936. In other words it was exiling the entire division.

The officers decided to make their move before they could be shunted off. They were often stirring up trouble, so the military police were not unprepared, but no one expected such a sudden move, and perhaps the heavy snows on the night before the incident also lulled people into a false sense of security. The snow was in fact fortuitous from the standpoint of the chief instigators, Captains Teruzō Andō and Shirō Nonaka and Lieutenant Yasuhide Kurihara, who had chosen February 26 some days before.

The day was picked because Captain Ichitarō Yamaguchi, who sympathized with the plot, would be the First Infantry Regiment's weekly duty officer on that day, as Andō would be for the Third Infantry Regiment. When the regimental commander went home at the end of the day, the weekly duty officer was the one left in charge of the regiment for the night.

At 3:00 A.M. on February 26, the two duty officers called together an emergency meeting of the various companies in their respective regiments. The troops had been aroused from a sound sleep, and they gathered hurriedly on the parade ground, still buttoning their uniforms. More than half of them were farmers' sons from country villages who had only entered the army a month or so before. They had suffered through the cold winter; they knew poverty and exploitation. They wholeheartedly concurred when their leaders read out the manifesto calling for a "Shōwa Restoration." But even if they didn't, they had been taught that their company commanders were their "fathers" and that "orders from a superior officer were the same as orders from the emperor," which they had to obey without question.

"We're conducting night maneuvers." "We're going to visit Yasukuni Shrine." These were the sorts of things the young soldiers were told as they left the barracks. They assumed they would be told the true nature of their mission on the way. No one hesitated. Morale was high.

These forces, including members of Third Regiment of the Imperial Guards and others, totaled over 1,400 men. Their primary objectives were to assassinate Prime Minister Keisuke Okada, Lord Keeper of the Privy Seal Makoto Saitō, Grand Chamberlain Kantarō Suzuki, Finance Minister Korekiyo Takahashi, and former lord keeper of the privy seal Nobuaki Makino, who was wintering at the time at the Yugawara Hot Springs, about sixty

70

miles west of Tokyo. They also aimed to take over army and Tokyo Metropolitan Police headquarters. Furthermore, they planned to kill General Jōtarō Watanabe, inspector general of military education, and occupy the offices of the *Asahi Newspaper*.

At the appointed hour of 5:00 A.M., they struck their various targets simultaneously, furiously firing machine guns and pistols and wielding sabers. Saitō, Takahashi, and then Watanabe were quickly killed. Prime Minister Okada was initially reported dead, and Chamberlain Suzuki was critically wounded. Takahashi had been riddled with forty-seven bullets and had died instantly, but on top of that the assassins slashed him with their sabers, leaving more than ten wounds on his body. On the other hand, thanks to quick thinking on the part of a hotel maid, Makino was able to escape into the hills behind the inn where he was staying.

Furthermore, the victim first thought to be Okada turned out to be his brother-in-law, Denzō Matsuo, a colonel in the army reserves. Lieutenant Kurihara, in charge of the attack on the prime minister, had never seen Okada except in photographs, and thus mistakenly killed Matsuo, who was roughly the same age and appearance as his brother-in-law. The prime minister himself had fled to the bath and then to a closet in the maid's quarters, where he hid for two days before being rescued. It was a monumental blunder as assassination attempts go.

It was about 5:30 A.M. when the first reports of the coup reached the palace. The emperor was not yet awake. When Chamberlain Karonji awoke him with the news, Hirohito responded with a contemptuous "So they've finally made their move." Outraged by the way the troops had slaughtered his most trusted advisers, all the while praising and using his name, the emperor had reached his limit. From that moment on, until the incident was finally resolved, Hirohito was implacable. One of his close personal retainers, Military Attaché Shigeru Honjō, was the first to sample the emperor's anger. Shortly thereafter, the war minister arrived at the palace with a report on the rebellion. He timidly approached Hirohito and said, "The conduct of these officers is indeed disgraceful; yet, it arises from their sincere devotion to Your Majesty and to the nation. It is hoped that Your Majesty will understand their feelings." At these words the emperor flushed with anger. He stated unequivocally, "They have murdered Our closest advisers. What possible justification can be found for the brutality these officers have shown, no matter what their motives? We order the immediate suppression of these rebels." Honjō, fearing that the word "rebels" might raise serious opposition among the military, broke in, saying, "Perhaps Your Majesty would reconsider using the word 'rebels.'" But the emperor was adamant: "Soldiers who act without Our orders are not Our soldiers: They are rebels."

Prime Minister Okada was believed dead, so Home Affairs Minister Fumio Gotō arranged for the resignation of the cabinet. When the emperor saw the war minister's letter of resignation with the others, he became even more furious. Earlier, at the time of an attempt on Hirohito's life, the minister in charge of public order had offered his resignation. But this time War Minister Yoshiyuki Kawashima, although he was the man who bore the political responsibility for the rebellion, submitted a letter of resignation which implied that he was ignorant of the planning behind the attempted coup. An entry in Honjō's diary shows how unhappy Hirohito was over this: "When His Majesty saw that the war minister, who bore the heaviest responsibility for the incident, had submitted his resignation, he said: 'Does the war minister think that this letter absolves him? It's this kind of thinking that makes the Army so bad.' " Hirohito was also indignant that although early reports of the revolt had reached the palace, Kawashima was late in coming there himself.

In fact, the various leaders of the military establishment, from Kawashima down, had been taken by surprise and even tried to play up to the rebel officers. Kawashima himself had issued a statement praising the revolt. He concluded it by saying, "The motives behind your uprising have been made clear to the emperor. We recognize that your acts are a manifestation of your loyalty to the state." Even General Sadao Araki, the doyen of the army, called the rebels "restoration troops," thus giving them some degree of credibility. Major General Tomoyuki Yamashita, Inspector General of Military Affairs, also backed the rebels. With this kind of support, the rebel officers were confident of success, at least through the evening of February 26.

Before dawn on the twenty-seventh the army high command, intimidated by the emperor's fury, finally declared martial law and ordered the evacuation of the vicinity of the Akasaka Sanno Hotel, which the rebels had made their base. But they still refused to take direct action against the rebel force; rather, they did their utmost to negotiate. Even Lieutenant-General Kashii, the officer in charge of enforcing martial law, was in sympathy with the rebels. He conveyed the emperor's command to them as follows: "All occupying troops must return to their original companies. These are His Majesty's orders." A close scrutiny of this statement reveals that, although he had been ordered to suppress the rebellion, he was openly working to protect the rebel officers. To be sure, persuasion would be a bloodless solution to the problem, but Hirohito, still greatly agitated, repeatedly summoned Honjō, pressing him with questions about the steps taken to deal with the rebels. "Have the troops mobilized yet? Has fighting broken out?" The aide equivocated, saying, "Well, Your Majesty, the area has not quite yet been evacuated. . . ." Honjō's evasions drew a cold look from the emperor, who admonished, "It is clear that the divisional commanders do not understand their duties. We shall summon the Imperial Guard and lead them Ourselves. That will quell the rebellion!"

What with the emperor's obvious anger, the rebel officers could sense that the situation was turning against them by the moment, but just when they were thinking that the uprising was over, they received encouraging news that gave them renewed hope. Prince Chichibu, the emperor's younger brother and the commander of the Eighth Division at Hirosaki, about 450 miles north of Tokyo, was rushing to the capital to provide reinforcements. He was on an express train at that very moment—so the news went. Before being transferred to Hirosaki, the prince had been stationed with the Third Regiment in Azabu. There he had taken a liking to Captain Andō, one of the rebel leaders. They shared an admiration of the work of the right-wing theorist Ikki Kita. Kita's *An Outline Plan for the Reconstruction of Japan,* published in 1923, had become the bible of all rightists and ultranationalist groups. The prince's sympathy for Kita's ideas and his natural authority won him the respect of the young troops. Indeed, just before the incident, the prince had jokingly asked one of the rebel officers, Lieutenant Sakai, to come and fetch him with his troops.

While the news that Chichibu was on his way to Tokyo gave new hope to the rebels, it caused consternation at the palace. The prince's announced intent was to visit the emperor, but if he were to back the rebels, it would be a serious blow. Vice-Minister of Foreign Affairs Mamoru Shigemitsu recalled later:

"We often heard soldiers criticize His Majesty, and at the time of the February 26 revolt, I will never forget how some dared suggest that if His Majesty opposed their reforms, they would turn to a certain imperial prince [Chichibu] and make him emperor."

As a last resort, the Imperial Household Ministry sent Professor Hiraizumi of the University of Tokyo as an envoy to the prince. He intercepted the prince's train at Minakami, and from there to Ueno Station in Tokyo he explained the situation to him in detail and implored him not to do anything rash. Hiraizumi was a well-known scholar who espoused the view that the emperor was an absolute ruler. He was popular among rightists, and for two and a half years he had taught the political history of Japan to Prince Chichibu. When they arrived at Ueno Station on the evening of the twenty-seventh a tight net of security was thrown around the area. Two trucks carrying contingents of the Imperial Guard were waiting. There was a fear that he might be kidnapped by supporters of the rebellion.

Arriving at the palace, Prince Chichibu first went to

speak with Chief Private Secretary to the Lord Keeper of the Privy Seal Kōichi Kido, who gave him the latest news. After he had finished, Kido urged the prince, "His Majesty is extremely worried. As a younger brother, a prince, to his elder brother, the emperor, please do what you can to help him."

"I shall stand by his side," promised the prince.

Next he met Prince Takamatsu, and after receiving one more update on the situation, he went in to see the emperor. No one knows what was said during the meeting, although the two did have a meal together, and it is clear that the prince pledged his full support to the emperor. It seems that Chichibu was angered by the brutality of the killings, which was out of keeping with the honor code that was supposed to govern the actions of a Japanese soldier.

With the question of Chichibu's loyalty settled, the emperor continued to press his aides for action in dealing with the rebels, but he only got evasive answers: "The evacuation of civilians takes time," or "We don't have adequate forces at hand and must wait for reinforcements." At this, Hirohito became indignant. "Are you telling me that if reinforcements do not arrive, we cannot begin a counterattack?" He wanted the incident settled even if it meant spilling the blood of his subjects, be they innocent civilians or common soldiers merely following orders.

Hirohito's insistence put the high command on the defensive, and they were forced to take action. Already some 25,000 troops from the Imperial Guard had surrounded the rebel headquarters. To signal their readiness to attack, they established machine-gun posts and drove tanks up and down the streets. The navy quickly assembled the First

Fleet in Tokyo Bay, with its guns aimed directly at the rebel positions. If the rebels continued to resist, they would no longer have the moral argument that they were acting on behalf of the emperor. On the contrary, they would be remembered as traitors, their honor forever stained. The young officers embraced one another tearfully. At Lieutenant Kurihara's suggestion, they requested the presence of an imperial messenger so that they might commit suicide, thereby bringing an honorable end to the affair. A weeping Major Yamashita went to the palace. He pleaded with Honjō to send an imperial messenger and let the men die with honor. Honjō reported in his diary:

> His Majesty is extremely angry. He said that if they wanted to commit suicide, they should go ahead and do it, but that sending an imperial representative is out of the question. Furthermore, he said that if the division commander has done nothing about the incident, it proves that he does not know where his duty lies. I had never heard His Majesty issue so stern a censure. He gave strict orders that the rebellion be suppressed immediately at any cost.

"Stern censure" and "at any cost" were indications of how strongly the emperor felt. A little later Honjō spoke to the emperor again about the matter of an imperial representative. He argued, "Even if we assume their actions were wrong, I believe they acted with single-minded devotion to the nation." But Hirohito would have none of it. He replied: "All you are saying is that they did not do it out of self-interest." When Hirohito categorically refused to send a messenger, the despairing rebel officers awoke to the reality of their situation. But even if they continued to disobey the emperor, they reasoned, their resistance served the higher cause of true loyalty and patriotism. They decided to continue the rebellion. At once they sent instructions to all rebel positions. Even the enlisted men were firm in their resolve to die honorably, and they prepared to take up arms once again.

It was at this point that the following notice was issued:

> Since it is not yet too late, return to your home units.
>
> Those who continue to resist are traitors, and will be shot.
>
> Your families will be treated as traitors; they weep for you.

NHK announcer Shigeru Nakamura, one of the most eloquent men of his generation, caused a precipitous drop in morale among the rebel troops when he delivered the following message in a voice choked with emotion:

> You may have believed that the orders from your superiors were right, and in obeying them absolutely, your motives were sincere. However, His Majesty the Emperor has commanded all of you to return to your home units. . . . You must not defy His Majesty for in doing so, you will be branded traitors for all time. Since even as I speak it is not too late, lay down your arms and return to your barracks. If you do so, your offenses will be pardoned.

It was the third day of the revolt, and the rebels were being worn down by the cold. Here and there, groups of soldiers began to drop out and return to their units, and the leaders made no move to stop them. The most senior officer, Captain Nonaka, committed suicide; the others surrendered, planning to continue the battle at their court-martial. Because the emperor had taken a stand and expressed his anger, the attempted coup was put down without bloodshed. Even afterward Hirohito maintained an unyielding stance toward the rebels. When the court-martial was convened, Hirohito warned: "Indecisiveness will only invite trouble. It is imperative that principled, forceful officers be appointed to be the judges and judge advocates." Nevertheless it was difficult to judge the merits of the case. The rebel officers belonged to a faction of the army known as the *kōdōha* (imperial way faction), whose main aim was to achieve a form of national socialism, in particular to address the plight of the rural poor, who made up roughly half of the population. They also advocated military preparedness against a feared Soviet invasion, and were sternly anti-Communist. When we consider that the invasion of China and the prosecution of the Pacific War was promoted by the *kōdōha*'s rival faction, the *tōseiha* (control faction), Japanese history might have taken a different course had the February 26 rebellion succeeded.

After the war, Hirohito, looking back on his own actions, said: "In some sense I was violating the constitution in my rebuke of Prime Minister Tanaka at the time of the Chang Tso-lin incident, and in the stand I took in the February 26 Incident." Indeed, his actions on these two occasions have forced us to reevaluate our long-standing view of the emperor as a gentle, conscientious man. At no other time in the eighty-eight years of his life had he ever shown such violent emotions. Nothing could better illustrate the two sides of Emperor Hirohito—the theoretically all-powerful "divine" ruler and the human being capable of dramatic displays of emotion.

The First Shot

On July 7, 1937, Japanese troops occupying northern China were on night maneuvers near the Marco Polo Bridge in the outskirts of Peking when they were shot at by Chinese forces. The Chinese soldiers were with the Twenty-ninth Army, China's finest.

Ever since the Manchurian Incident, anti-Japanese sentiment had been growing, and for the Japanese troops the situation had become quite precarious. The North China Occupation Army had achieved its status as an occupying force at the time of the Boxer Rebellion in 1900. It acted in concert with the Kwantung Army in actively pursuing total domination of North China. Eight months earlier, in November of 1936, Hideki Tōjō, then Kwantung Army chief of staff, organized a Mongol-run independent regime in Chahar Province in Inner Mongolia, and had the Chinese Nationalist army expelled.

The few shots that were actually fired at the Marco Polo Bridge had enormous repercussions, and even though no one was injured, the leaders of the North China Occupation

81

Army jumped on the skirmish as a chance to make their move militarily. They proceeded immediately to rout the Nationalists from the area, then, in a very threatening manner, pressed the Chinese for concessions. But the Chinese side was in no mood to compromise. It was one thing for the Japanese to occupy Manchuria or Mongolia, but this time they had struck into China proper, and were just outside the ancient capital of Peking. The Chinese vowed to resist to the very end.

Tensions grew day by day, but arrayed against Japan's several thousand troops was an enormous Chinese force. The Twenty-ninth Army alone, China's main force, numbered over 80,000. Back in Japan, the army quickly ordered reinforcements in by boat from Hiroshima.

The emperor asked by way of warning: "Isn't this the Manchurian Incident all over again?" He was also concerned about how the Soviet Union would react to a large Japanese military presence in China. He put the question to his cousin, Chief of Staff Prince Kan'in, who replied, "The Army says the Soviets will do nothing."

"That's just the Army's opinion. But what would happen if the Soviets *did* take some sort of action?" Hirohito reiterated the question, but Kan'in could not give him a satisfactory answer.

Still, the emperor was wavering. After all, unlike in the Manchurian Incident, this time the Chinese had fired first. What would be the point of trying to keep the army too much in check? In addition, three days earlier, War Minister Gen Sugiyama had assured him, "We'll have this matter all taken care of in a month." So this time Hirohito did not press the military further.

However, Sugiyama's "one month" proved to be a ridiculous estimate. The Chinese, united behind Chiang Kai-shek's Kuomintang, were filled with a new fighting spirit. For a time they seemed willing to negotiate a cease-fire, but Japan's demands were too far-reaching: Both sides were working at cross purposes, and the talks broke down. The incident proceeded to develop into a full-scale conflict.

In August 1937 the fighting had reached central China. The Japanese army captured the former nationalist capital of Nanking, where they committed one of the most infamous atrocities of the China war, later known as the Rape of Nanking. The Chinese had already moved their government deeper inland, to the city of Hankow, and proclaimed a scorched-earth policy of resistance. This shattered any expectations the Japanese may have had of a quick end to the war.

In response to the prospects of a long-term conflict, a military headquarters was set up in the imperial palace, and inevitably the emperor was kept very busy. Night and day he was beset by worries over the outcome of the military action, and began to look haggard. Hirohito was a man of delicate sensibilities. Worry soon took its toll, and as he so often did in such circumstances, he began talking to himself. Sometimes, when reports from the field were good, he would feel even more exhausted—perhaps due to the sudden release of tension.

His aides were concerned and suggested he go to the imperial residences at Hayama or Nasu for a rest, but as one of them said later, "His Majesty was very scrupulous in his duties, and although we urged him to take a rest, he was reluctant to do so." Perhaps his reluctance stemmed from an embarrassing incident that had occurred at the time of the outbreak of hostilities between Japan and China. Hirohito had gone to Hayama for some relaxation and to pursue his interests in marine biology. Although he received reports of the Marco Polo Bridge Incident, he did not return to Tokyo immediately. Instead, he remained in Hayama for three days, much to the disgust of certain factions within the military.

There was some grumbling, though nothing more serious than "Imagine! For the emperor to be fooling around with worthless little animals at such a crucial time!" and "If he has so much free time, I wish he'd spend it learning more about military matters. . . ."

It seemed, then, that Hirohito's "reluctance" was a reluctance to get involved with the military. But thereafter he virtually gave up the research and experiments that he conducted with so much obvious pleasure. "It is my only hobby," he'd once said in his defense.

Still, from time to time he would summon his old biology mentor, Professor Hattori, to the palace, and would at least have a chance to listen to his lectures.

***

A year after hostilities began in China, something that Japan had been most concerned about occurred: a skirmish with Soviet troops. It took place at Changkufeng, close to the meeting point of the Soviet, Manchurian, and Korean borders, when Russian troops took up positions in disputed territory. Japanese troops stationed in the area leapt rashly into action, under the pretext that (as one officer put it) "faced with these moves on the part of the Soviet Union while Japan is locked in an extended conflict with China, we should respond and use it as an opportunity to test our fighting ability, while limiting the fighting to the Changkufeng area."

The central command, however, took a more cautious stand. It was a crucial moment in the China campaign, as Japanese troops had just advanced on the capital, Hankow, so the generals in Tokyo were hesitant about getting involved in an extended clash with the Russians. But they succumbed to the arguments of the troops in the field, who maintained that the rugged mountains and hemmed-in terrain of the Changkufeng area posed no problem, and who further insisted that the Soviet designs on the area posed a serious military threat to Japan. They also pointed out that an engagement there would give the Japanese troops a chance to test themselves. It seemed to those in the field that a firm military response could only bring good results.

Japan's "Korean Army" was in high spirits and ready for battle. Just as they were about to depart for the war zone, however, an emergency message arrived, canceling their previous orders. What had happened was this: The war minister and the chief of staff had gone separately to the palace to report to the emperor on the plans. Hirohito, guessing that they wanted permission to make use of the "Korean Army," said to his military attaché: "If they ask me for permission to use military force, I am not inclined to do so. So if that is the purpose of their visit, do not let them into the palace."

But the two asked for an audience nonetheless, and the emperor had no choice but to comply. When Chief of Staff

Prince Kan'in came to the palace and heard from the attaché what Hirohito had said, he gave up and left. Unaware of all this, War Minister Seishirō Itagaki showed up late, gained an audience with Hirohito, and proceeded to argue forcefully for the necessity of applying military force against the Soviets.

The emperor asked him, "What do the ministers concerned have to say?"

"Both the foreign minister and the navy minister concur with this assessment" was the reply.

In fact, both ministers did agree with the *deployment* of troops, but Hirohito also knew that they were adamantly opposed to those troops using force. And since Itagaki looked as though he were going to brazenly fail to mention that fact, the emperor became very upset and took the war minister to task: "Really, the Army's behavior is outrageous! Be it at Lukouchiao at the time of the Manchurian Incident, or just recently at the Marco Polo Bridge, they ignore the orders sent out by central command and all too often go their own way, employing despicable, inexcusable methods. They are Our forces, yet We find their conduct disgraceful, not to say impertinent." And he added, "Henceforth not one soldier will be moved without Our explicit orders."

Itagaki, shaken by the emperor's severe reprimand, took his leave, saying, "I can never enter His Majesty's presence again. I must resign."

Prince Kan'in joined him in announcing his resignation, saying: "As a senior leader of the Army, I am no longer fit to advise His Majesty."

Feeling that Hirohito had overstepped his constitutional

bounds once more, Prime Minister Konoe intervened and placated the emperor, who gave the order, "Let the war minister and chief of staff continue their duties as before." At this, the two men withdrew their resignations.

The whole incident was almost a reenactment of the scene between Hirohito and Prime Minister Tanaka ten years before, when the emperor had said, "I do not want to see him again," and had thereby precipitated the resignation of the entire cabinet. This time, too, it seems that Hirohito had been rather hasty. To be sure, he had stepped beyond the bounds of a constitutional monarch, but the army's attitude had become so arrogant that perhaps such forcefulness was necessary.

In the end, after a series of clashes around Changkufeng, the army followed Hirohito's will and withdrew, offering virtually no resistance. The Soviets pursued them, inflicting heavy casualties. About a month after hostilities had commenced, the two sides negotiated a truce.

***

In May of 1939, less than six months after Changkufeng, another clash erupted between Japan and the Soviet Union. At Nomonhan, on the border between Manchuria and Outer Mongolia, Mongolian troops, backed by the Soviets, suddenly invaded Manchurian territory.

The Nomonhan region is a vast, undulating grassy plain, with few natural features to demarcate national borders. When Manchuria declared independence as the state of Manchukuo, the Manchurian government designated the Halha River as the border, but now the Mongolians were eating into that territory. The Soviets' aim was clearly to reconnoiter, as well as to divert Japanese troops from the China front. Central command warned the Kwantung Army not to fall into the trap, but to no avail. The infamous outfit reacted rashly to the incursion. Figuring that the Soviet-Mongolian supply line would be vulnerable since it ran through a long range of mountains, they decided they would teach the Russians a lesson with a show of force. What began as a clash between Manchurian and Mongolian troops soon escalated into a deadly serious fight between Soviet and Japanese forces. Both parties threw airplanes, tanks, and heavy artillery into what became a full-scale battle.

The Soviets, with several thousand trucks to carry personnel, had a significant advantage over the Kwantung Army, which had far poorer transportation capabilities. Moreover, arrayed in this land battle against an overwhelming force of Soviet tanks and heavy artillery was a Japanese army consisting mainly of foot-weary infantrymen. It was Japan's "flesh" against the other side's "steel." Frustrated at their powerlessness, the Japanese withdrew to the banks of the Halha River.

However, the one thing the Japanese did have in their favor was superior air power. Their surprise attack on the Soviet air base at Tomsk, in which they destroyed some 120 planes with a loss of just four of their own, was an eye-opening encounter. The air base at Tomsk was located 100 kilometers (60 miles) inside Outer Mongolian territory, so to strike at it risked escalating a minor border skirmish into a real war. Central command was therefore opposed, but the Kwantung Army acted on its own.

Although Hirohito felt that the tail was now wagging the dog as far as the military went, due to the seriousness of the battle, and its outcome, he did not openly display his displeasure. He remarked rather mildly, "The Kwantung Army command will be more cautious in the future, and surely they will take some sort of disciplinary action." Perhaps he had half given up by then.

After four months of fighting, the Nomonhan Incident ended in crushing defeat for Japan. The dead and missing totaled some 20,000, with another 20,000 wounded. Virtually all the regimental commanders who participated either died in battle or committed suicide. Furthermore, when the emperor's uncle, Prince Higashikuni, disappeared for a time during the fighting, his aide, feeling responsible, took his own life. It was truly a debacle for Japan. Among other things, the Japanese had badly underestimated Soviet military might, which the impressive Russian superiority in tanks and other armored vehicles had graphically demonstrated.

Hirohito at Home

Among signs of great change in the world, the emperor had his own personal worries. One of his sovereign duties was to produce an heir to the throne that had, by tradition, been "an unbroken line of ten thousand generations." But there had so far been no hopeful indications. The empress had only borne him daughters: Princess Teru Shigeko in December 1925, Princess Hisa Sachiko in September 1927, Princess Taka Kazuko in September 1929, and Princess Yori Atsuko in March 1931. Hirohito's distress was acute, especially in light of his responsibility to his ancestors.

In an age when many people believed that the failure to produce a crown prince was a bad omen for Japan, there was casual public debate, with some suggesting simplistically that the problem was because "the empress is only capable of producing daughters," or "Emperor Meiji had some twenty consorts, but the emperor has only one."

Prince Saionji and Lord Keeper of the Privy Seal Count Nobuaki Makino were getting on in years, and they had grown especially impatient with the imperial couple's failure to produce a son. One of them said, "We need to think about this problem seriously. We cannot rely on the emperor and empress to solve it." The two elder statesmen must have felt very strongly about the matter to take such an unusual responsibility upon themselves. They summoned the most beautiful court ladies, ordered them to pay special attention to their makeup and dress seductively, and generally prepared them should the emperor be inclined to visit their quarters. There is also a story, possibly apocryphal, about Hirohito being sent photographs of three lovely, beautifully attired young ladies of good family in hopes that he would find one of them attractive. Saying simply, "They all seem to be such nice young ladies, I hope that each makes a suitable marriage for herself," the emperor returned the photographs.

It would not be fair to criticize Saionji and Makino for their scheming in this matter. Historically it was actually the exception rather than the rule for the empress to bear the crown prince. In fact, the previous three emperors, Taishō, Meiji, and Kōmei, all had ladies-in-waiting as their natural mothers. For a man like Saionji, born before the Meiji Restoration, there was nothing particularly odd about turning to a concubine in such a situation.

And indeed, the emperor was just past thirty, and by no means without human feelings. One close associate has claimed that there was one beautiful court lady of good birth who seems to have caught the emperor's eye. He would invite her to play chess with him, or summon her to his apartments for a chat. In fact, another highly placed court lady was heard to complain, "His Majesty seems only to have eyes for *her*." Of course, he spent most of his time with

Empress Nagako, and she seems to have kept a close eye on him. In any case, the presumed "affair" didn't amount to anything, and the lady in question left the court shortly afterward.

Nevertheless, the empress herself must have been feeling a terrible burden. Not only had her marriage to Hirohito been opposed, but now she did not seem able to bear him an heir. The emperor tried to comfort her, saying, "It does not matter to me. There's always Prince Chichibu and Prince Takamatsu."

It seems likely, however, that these words only made her feel worse. But the alternative—for Hirohito to take a concubine—would have been even more unpleasant for the empress as a woman. And from the standpoint of the nation, there was some resistance to the heir to the throne coming from outside the family. Furthermore, Prince Chichibu and Prince Takamatsu had yet to produce their own heirs. And the late Emperor Taishō's fourth son, Prince Mikasa, was only seventeen.

Such was the situation when in early summer of 1933 the empress became pregnant again, for the sixth time. (It is not generally known that, in 1932, Nagako had a miscarriage, so this was, in fact, her sixth pregnancy, not her fifth, as was widely believed.)

The nation felt mixed emotions—hoping for the best, fearing the worst—but as always, many went to pray at shrines and temples. As December 28, the projected date of birth, drew near, sirens were set up in key locations throughout the land to notify people of the outcome. The signal was to be a single minute-long blast if a girl were born, followed by a second minute-long blast ten seconds later if it were a boy.

However, five days earlier than forecast, on December 23, the silence of the cloudless early morning sky over Japan was shattered by the wail of sirens. People were startled and after sixty seconds, as the sirens fell silent, everyone waited anxiously, wondering if there would be a second blast. It was a ten-second eternity, but suddenly the sirens sounded again. The feelings of the whole nation were expressed by Kōichi Kido, chief private secretary to the lord keeper of the privy seal, in his diary: "At last we hear two blasts of the siren. Finally the nation's fervent desire has been fulfilled, the great problem has been solved. I am so filled with emotion at this moment, I cannot stop the tears."

Following the birth of Crown Prince Akihito, a second son, Prince Hitachi, was born in 1935. He was followed in 1939 by a fifth daughter, Princess Suga Takako. In all the imperial couple raised seven healthy children.

However, in accordance with imperial household custom, the crown prince, at the age of three years and three months, was moved to the Akasaka Detached Palace, while his brother was moved to the Aoyama Palace when he reached the same age. The four older princesses resided in the Kuretake Pavilion from the time they were of school age. Only their youngest daughter, Princess Suga, lived in the main palace apartments with her parents. Several reasons are usually given for this practice of separating imperial parents and children. One is that since each family member has his or her own attendants, it is simply too cumbersome to have them all in one residence. Furthermore, such close arrangements might hinder the children's upbringing. Besides, there was so much coming and going at the main palace.

93

Prince Saionji, in a memorandum to the throne, made an especially stern case for raising the crown prince in separate quarters, advising: "The one who is to become emperor must, for the good of the nation, necessarily forgo the normal parent-child relationship."

But even when the imperial children lived with their parents, it was not "living together" in the usual sense of the word. Indeed, they might as well have been living apart, since within the palace compound, the emperor, the empress, and the children each occupied separate apartments, with only long corridors connecting them. It was hardly a typical family home.

Each prince and princess was assigned a chamberlain and a lady-in-waiting who acted as surrogate parents. Their daily lives were carried on apart from the rest of the family. They only came in contact with their mother and father in the morning and evening, when they visited the emperor's apartments and made formal greetings. Also, when the emperor left the palace on business, they were permitted to go out and see him off—indeed, this was one of the few small pleasures the children had to look forward to.

On a morning in April 1940, as he was on his way to his first day at the Peers' School, Akihito appeared for his morning greetings smartly dressed in a naval uniform. Hirohito looked at him proudly. "Listen to your teachers, and do your best," he said by way of advice.

Unfortunately, the empress was bedridden with a cold, but as the palace sickroom was just across a small courtyard from the emperor's apartments, a lady-in-waiting took the young prince over by the window so that she could see him. The empress, moved to tears at the sight of her handsome young son dressed for his first day of school, waved for a long time across the courtyard, not stopping until she was sure he had seen her.

Hirohito, though generally healthy, nonetheless caught two or three colds a year. Whenever he was confined to the sickroom, the empress would take along knitting or something to read and would keep him company, now tending to him, now chatting, staying by his side as long as she could. It seems unnecessary to reiterate how harmonious their marriage was. Perhaps their success was due more than anything to the empress's bright yet gentle nature, and the emperor's own spotless character. Although in interests and personality they were virtual opposites, they complemented each other beautifully, which accounted for the depth of their love for one another.

In addition to botany and marine biology, Hirohito's interests included playing cards and Japanese chess, while the empress's tastes ran in the opposite direction, toward things in which her husband had no interest, such as Western classical music, piano, No chanting, Japanese painting, and calligraphy. In terms of personality, too, the two were quite different. In contrast to Nagako, who was open and talkative, Hirohito was reticent, methodical, somewhat awkward, and not particularly witty. Even in eating habits, they differed. The emperor preferred fattier foods like eel, tempura, and Chinese cooking, and would not touch alcohol, while the empress liked lighter Japanese dishes and would occasionally have a drink. When she had a cold, she liked to drink a mixture of saké and raw egg. Even when she was not ill, her ladies-in-waiting would, without being asked, sometimes make her a drink when she looked tired, and she would always finish it with great enjoyment. She also drank wine from time to time; indeed, being something of a drinker, she was particularly fond of a speciality from her mother's home town of Kagoshima, *ojushi*, which consisted of sushi dipped in strong local saké.

If there was anything the couple agreed on, it was that they both had a weakness for sweet things, although for a time the empress used artificial sweeteners to help control her weight.

It is common knowledge that Hirohito enjoyed Japanese chess, but his fondness for mah-jongg, which in Japan has an unsavory reputation as a gamblers' game, was a better-kept secret. It seems that once, in the early Shōwa years, the palace chamberlain smuggled a mah-jongg set in to the emperor, who took to the game quickly. The emperor and empress would sometimes play it with the gentlemen- and ladies-in-waiting of the palace, and the young princess would join them too. Empress Nagako more or less knew the game already, but for the princess it was new. The emperor patiently explained the rules to her and soon she was making progress. It is amusing to try and picture how these palace mah-jongg games went, but in any case mah-jongg and Emperor Hirohito were a combination that few people would ever have imagined.

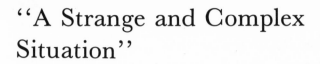

"A Strange and Complex Situation"

In the early months of 1939, Hitler, in an attempt to break free of the constraints of the Treaty of Versailles, which had held Germany in check since World War I, and to provide an effective counter to the Soviet Union, England, France, and the United States, conceived of an alliance of Japan, Germany, and Italy. Japan and Germany had already signed the Anti-Comintern Pact in 1936, promising to protect each other from Soviet aggression, but for the three nations to step beyond this and conclude a military agreement was even more significant. With this pact they would become a major force in global politics. For Japan, in particular, it meant an irreversible commitment to expansionism.

Until just ten years before, Japan had viewed England and the United States as its best friends on the international scene, but as the military gained influence in domestic matters, alliances began to shift. First gradually, then more rapidly, Japan moved closer to Italy and Germany. The nations of the world again seemed headed toward a confrontation between the "haves" and the "have-nots." Still, there was some risk involved in allying with totalitarian nations like Italy and Germany, who disregarded international conventions and for whom loyalty was quickly forgotten like a worn-out shoe. One misstep, and Japan might well be destroyed.

The army and rightists vigorously promoted a tripartite alliance, while the navy and liberals just as staunchly opposed it. With public opinion divided and little prospect for a resolution, the cabinet just waited on the sidelines.

Seeing his own government's hesitation, Japan's military attaché in Berlin, Lieutenant-General Hiroshi Ōshima, took drastic steps. An admirer of Hitler, he saw to it that only favorable reports of Germany were sent back to Japan. He challenged virtually every central directive from the foreign affairs ministry, and even took it upon himself to promise the Germans that Japan would fight on their side should they go to war with England and the United States.

The emperor found his unauthorized excesses unpardonable. "Perhaps we should call in the war minister to reprimand him," he suggested to his chief administrative aide, Kōichi Kido, chief private secretary to the lord keeper of the privy seal.

The latter replied, "I suspect that to draw attention to the situation by reprimanding him would only make matters worse. I think it would be better just to leave things the way they are."

This placated Hirohito for a while, but later, when War Minister Itagaki came to the palace on some other business, the emperor caught sight of him and was unable to hold back: "Is it not a usurpation of imperial authority for the military attaché to promise, on his own, our military cooperation with Germany? I am further disturbed by the fact that the Army seems to support him on this issue, and I am displeased that you have failed to bring the matter up at cabinet meetings.''

In the end, Hitler, ever full of tricks, temporarily shelved his plans for an alliance with the Japanese, who seemed unable to come to any sort of decision regarding the Tripartite Alliance. He did a complete turnabout and signed a nonaggression pact with the enemy—the Soviet Union! It was an unlikely alliance, but it nevertheless dramatically changed the complexion of world politics and derailed negotiations for a tripartite agreement.

A shocked Prime Minister Kiichirō Hiranuma resigned his post with the famous parting words "The situation in Europe has taken a strange and complex new turn."

***

When appointing General Nobuyuki Abe as the next prime minister, the emperor expressed his displeasure with the army's brash behavior, and made the following firm stipulation: "Either Umezu or Hata [who was the emperor's military attaché at the time] must be appointed war minister. No matter if the three Army chiefs [i.e., the war minister, the chief of staff, and the inspector-general of military education] propose someone else for the post: I am not inclined to go along with them."

And he added, with uncharacteristic forcefulness, "In foreign affairs, our goal should be maintaining a harmonious relationship with England and the United States. Furthermore, the foreign minister should act in a manner more clearly consistent with constitutional provisions."

In addition, he made specific recommendations for the posts of finance, home, and justice ministers.

According to an account by Kurahei Yuasa, then lord keeper of the privy seal, Abe "flushed deeply as if he'd drunk a glass of vinegar; red blotches came out all over his face," and he took his leave.

Moreover, when Hirohito read unsubstantiated stories in the newspapers that Lieutenants-General Isogai, Tada, and Yanagawa had all been mentioned as candidates for the post of war minister, his reaction, according to Hata, was "extremely vehement": "We cannot agree to any of those three. The appointee must be someone upon whom We can rely."

At this point the army proposed Hata for the position. Of course, the emperor had gone rather too far in intervening so forcefully in the appointment of cabinet ministers. Yet, the fact that he expressed his likes and dislikes, in terms of individuals, so clearly, and that he felt he had to overstep his bounds in this matter, shows just how completely the military had insinuated itself into political affairs.

***

The nonaggression pact with the Soviet Union gave Hitler virtually free rein in Europe. After invading Poland, Germany continued its advance into France in May 1940, quickly occupying Paris. The British expeditionary force pulled back to Dunkirk, from where it was evacuated to England. Italy, which had been waiting and watching, plunged into the war on Germany's side. Germany's ultimate victory looked virtually assured, and in Japan, calls for a Tripartite Alliance, which had died down the previous year, were voiced again, joined ardently by Foreign Affairs Minister Yōsuke Matsuoka. Matsuoka had been Japan's ambassador plenipotentiary when Japan had withdrawn from the League of Nations. He was a garrulous man with a strong personality. The army, under War Minister Hideki Tōjō, was strongly in favor of the alliance, and even the more cautious navy eventually became an enthusiastic supporter.

The navy's interest was easily explained. Since Germany now occupied the Netherlands, it controlled Dutch interests in the Pacific area, most importantly the Dutch East Indies (now Indonesia), a source of oil, tin, rubber, and rice—all materials essential to the prosecution of war. The navy wanted to ensure access to these resources.

The proponents of the alliance felt pressed. They feared that if German victory seemed assured before an alliance was concluded, the Germans would no longer need the Japanese and would send them packing. But it seems that Hitler was also in favor of an alliance. To encourage them, he dispatched Special Envoy Heinrich Stahmer to Tokyo as his personal representative.

The emperor was cautious: "Even if we wait to see what happens between Germany and Russia, there will still be time for an alliance." On another occasion he said, "Surely the United States will embargo imports of oil and scrap iron to Japan by way of retaliation. What will happen to Japan then?"

But the rest of Japan had become totally fascinated by Germany, and most people wanted Japan to take the step.

On September 19, 1940, at a meeting attended by the emperor, Japan formally joined the alliance, thus committing itself to a fateful course.

Hirohito, discouraged, was heard muttering to himself, "No matter how you look at it, this will be ruinous for the Army. They won't wake up to the situation until Manchuria and Korea have been lost." In fact, in five short years his anxious prediction would come true.

The army and navy were interested in more than just the Dutch East Indies. They were also poised to occupy French Indochina (now Vietnam). One of the reasons that the Sino-Japanese War had dragged on for so long was that England and the United States were providing the Chinese with a steady supply of arms and ammunition, and that supply route ran straight through Vietnam into China's Yunan Province. Besides, French Indochina would provide an ideal advance base for Japanese incursions into the Malay Peninsula, Singapore, and the Dutch East Indies, and with France now under the thumb of Germany, it seemed like a perfect opportunity to strike. Under the prodding of the military, the Japanese government pressured the Vichy regime into permitting Japanese troops to occupy the northern part of Indochina. The emperor found this approach cowardly, and said with a frown, "I don't want our nation to be playing the bully like Frederick the Great or Napoleon. We must not be Machiavellian. Let us never forget the spirit of harmony that has been part of us since the ancient past, that spirit expressed in the phrase 'The eight corners of the world under one roof.'"

Just as Hirohito had predicted, the Japanese occupation of French Indochina brought quick retaliation from the

United States in the form of an iron and steel embargo. Today Japan is a steel exporter, but in those days it relied on the United States for more than half of its oil and iron needs, so the embargo was a severe blow. For its part, England reopened the Burma Road, the supply route to Chiang Kai-shek's army through Burma, which it had earlier closed because of Japanese pressure. This put Japan in a precarious position. Like it or not, the war in China could not be won now unless Japan took control of the Malay Peninsula and the Dutch East Indies.

***

The Japanese found themselves in completely new circumstances after they joined the Tripartite Alliance and occupied northern French Indochina. They struggled along in the war with China, but Chiang Kai-shek was convinced that ultimate victory would be his, and there seemed to be no prospect for a peaceful settlement.

When the pro-Japanese Wang Ching-wei, who saw himself as the national savior who would bring peace to China, defected from the Nationalists and fled the capital of Chungking, the Japanese leapt at what they saw as a fortunate opportunity. They set him up at the head of a puppet government, then concluded a peace treaty with the new regime. Wang's administration was really only over territory that Japan already controlled, so the ''peace'' was just a localized one. A larger peace was slipping further and further away. Moreover, Japan needed to support his government and ensure adequate food supplies. Doing this meant stretching supply lines to the limit, and Japan found itself shouldering a very heavy burden.

In January 1941, Hirohito summoned Gen Sugiyama, then chairman of the joint chiefs of staff, for a consultation. He asked, "Regarding the China situation, haven't you found a better solution than the policy you outlined earlier?" But none was forthcoming.

Sugiyama's notes on the meeting said, "His Majesty was not in a very bright mood. He would not even acknowledge my bow. I immediately felt an unusual atmosphere in the room."

Even the normally impartial Hirohito apparently had his likes and dislikes when it came to people, and he seemed to have negative feelings toward this General Sugiyama, as well as Generals Kawashima and Mazaki, who had been involved in the February 26 Incident. Likewise, he did not care much for former prime minister General Giichi Tanaka, nor for the former palace attaché Lieutenant-General Usami.

In April, Foreign Affairs Minister Matsuoka went to Berlin to ratify the Tripartite Alliance. He returned to Japan by way of the Trans-Siberian Railroad and stopped in Moscow to conclude a neutrality pact with the Soviet Union. People back in Japan were surprised by this sudden and unexpected move, yet also relieved that the threat from the north had been nullified for the time being.

Two months later, however, they were horrified when reports of Germany's invasion of Russia reached Japan. Two years earlier, Hiranuma had resigned as prime minister, lamenting the "strange and complex situation in Europe" after the conclusion of a nonaggression pact between Germany and the Soviet Union. And now those same two nations were at war with each other! While it certainly prompted people to reevaluate whether Hitler and Germany could be trusted, it was excellent news for Japan's plans to expand southward.

The ever ambitious militarists had their eye on occupying the southern part of French Indochina. Through Lord Keeper of the Privy Seal Kido, Hirohito expressed his displeasure at the army's repeated demands for action. He stated, "I am not at all pleased when you act on your own, and take advantage of the other side's weaknesses like a thief at a fire. However, in order to deal with the unsettled conditions we find in the world today, it would not do to be beaten because we failed to attack when we had the chance . . . . I only hope you will show prudence in the execution of your plans."

It appeared that Hirohito was beginning to sense the futility of continuing to resist the army's repeated demands. In July he finally acquiesced: "I worry about what this will do to our international reputation, but I guess it is all right to proceed. . . ."

The United States immediately froze Japanese assets held in America and announced an embargo on all goods to Japan except for raw cotton and foodstuffs. Subsequently England, the Netherlands, the Philippines, and New Zealand followed America's lead, leaving Japan with not a drop of oil to import.

Negotiations with the United States, going on since spring, had ended in deadlock. Konoe was more than ever searching for a breakthrough, proposing among other things a top-level summit, but in fact the countries were too far apart for that. Braced for the consequences, the

Japanese were standing at a crucial crossroads, and for better or for worse they felt they had no choice but to move into Southeast Asia.

The army was more determined than ever and began making preparations. A conference attended by cabinet members and officers from imperial headquarters put forward the "Outline for the Execution of National Policy." On September 6, at a meeting before the emperor, the plans were formally adopted.

When, as was customary, Hirohito had been shown the plans for review beforehand, he had expressed his concern to Prime Minister Konoe: "Judging from these plans, the first priority is preparation for war. Diplomatic negotiations are relegated to second place. I get the feeling that war is the master, diplomacy the slave. What do you think?"

He explicitly ordered, "War preparations and diplomacy should not be given equal footing. Diplomatic efforts must take precedence."

He then summoned Chairman of the Joint Chiefs of Staff Sugiyama and questioned him at length regarding the southern campaign and its prospects. Sugiyama told him, "So long as it is only Southeast Asia, we can settle the matter in about three months."

The emperor's reply was sharp: "You were war minister when the China Incident broke out and at that time you told me it would be settled within a month. Now it is four years later, and it is still going on, is it not?"

Sugiyama's excuse was that China's interior was so vast, but Hirohito pressed him further: "You say China's interior is vast. Tell me, is not the Pacific Ocean even bigger? What makes you so sure it will only take three months?"

Sugiyama could only hang his head in silence. But the emperor was by no means finished. He wanted to know more about the army's plans. "Are you absolutely certain you can win?" he demanded.

"I cannot say 'absolutely,' but I can say that in all probability we can win. However, it is impossible to be sure," Sugiyama equivocated.

"I see!" the emperor said in an uncharacteristically strong voice.

The next day, the sixth, Hirohito arrived early at the meeting. He motioned to Kido and asked, "I thought that I would like to say something at the meeting today. What do you think?"

Ordinarily at such meetings the emperor would not speak. He was there simply to listen as the others at the meeting asked and answered questions among themselves. (At this particular meeting, the other participants were the prime minister, the foreign minister, the finance minister, the war minister, the head of the cabinet planning board, the chairman of the joint chiefs of staff, the head of the general naval staff, and the head of the privy council.) But this time Hirohito was concerned that the military members of the meeting would dominate, making it all too easy for the group to decide to go to war—a course that would have a grave impact on the future of Japan.

Kido, however, discouraged him from speaking, saying, "I have arranged for Hara, the head of the privy council, to ask questions that will reflect Your Majesty's concerns." He added, "It would be all right for Your Majesty to end the meeting with these words of advice: 'Since the decisions made at this meeting are such as to risk the serious consequence of war, I hope that the high command will cooperate to the fullest in seeking a successful diplomatic solution to the situation.' ''

At the meeting the head of the cabinet planning board elaborated on the "Outline for the Execution of National Policy," stressing two points:

(1) In order to preserve the empire's self-sufficiency and self-defense, Japan was determined not to back away from war with the United States, Britain, and the Netherlands; consequently, war preparations were to be completed by the end of October.

(2) Parallel with the above, and in an effort to satisfy the emperor's demands, Japan would exhaust all diplomatic means with respect to the United States and England.

After his explanation, he went on to seek from the conference approval of the proposition that if Japan's demands were not met by the middle of October, the country should mobilize for war.

As planned, at this point Hara began his questioning on behalf of the emperor. It fell to Navy Minister Koshirō Oikawa to field the questions. Rather than a government minister like Oikawa, one would have expected either of the members of the high command, whose job it was to plan military strategy, to address in detail the queries, but they remained silent and gave no sign regarding their opinions.

Hirohito, face flushed bright red, stared hard at Oikawa. It seems his patience had snapped. Wiping at his fogged-over glasses with the thumbs of his white-gloved hands, he fixed a fierce gaze on his two military chiefs and said in a loud voice, "I find Mr. Hara's questions quite to the point. Why is it that the military chiefs have not seen fit to offer even a word in reply? It is most regrettable."

The plain truth was, until now every time the military chiefs of staff or the war minister had gone to the palace, they had ended up being taken to task by the emperor. This time they had hoped to avoid being berated by leaving it to the navy minister to make their case. They had not counted on Hirohito deciding to speak at all at the meeting, much less on his being so forceful. Everyone gulped.

The emperor slowly, deliberately, placed his hand in the right pocket of his suit and pulled out a slip of paper that he had prepared beforehand. In a clear, strong voice, he recited the following poem twice through:

> I believed this was a world
> In which all men were brothers.
> Across the four seas
> Why then do the waves and winds
> Arise now in such turmoil?

Then he added, "This poem by the Meiji Emperor is one which I have always loved. That great emperor's love for peace is a feeling I have also held as my own."

Everyone in the room fell silent, shocked as if they had been touched by a live wire. At length the two military chiefs stood up one right after the other and assured Hirohito that they would make a diplomatic solution their first priority and would only resort to war should all else fail.

Thus one last desperate effort was made to negotiate with the United States, but America proved immovable in its own demands. In the face of the military's insistence that there was now no other course but war, Konoe had to dissolve his cabinet and resign.

On October 17, at a meeting of senior statesmen, all former prime ministers, Kido proposed then war minister Tōjō as the next prime minister, stating, "What we need now more than anything else is to reexamine the decisions of the September 6 conference with the support of both the army and the navy." In fact, the decision was virtually Kido's alone. The various elders assembled were in no position to express their own opinions. And with that, the fateful tenure of Tōjō as prime minister began. He assumed the post on October 18, 1941.

In his diary, Kido wrote the following:

> With regards to the cabinet reorganization and the great efforts it involved, I received kind words of encouragement from His Majesty, and am truly grateful. There is great concern that should there be a single misstep with this new cabinet we will be propelled into senseless war. After careful deliberation, I believe that this [nomination of Tōjō for prime minister] is the only course that will result in new movement, and I have so informed the emperor, stating my position in detail. . . . His Majesty understood my reasoning easily. I was greatly moved when he said, "It is just as they say, you can't catch a tiger if you don't enter its lair."

After the war, of course, Kido was criticized for having proposed Tōjō for the post.

When he took office, Tōjō dispatched Saburō Kurusu, an experienced foreign-service officer, to assist then ambassador Kichisaburō Nomura with negotiations in Washington.

110

Back home he convened a liaison conference with the government and military leaders in hopes of moving the country in a new direction. But as Japan was unwilling to make any concessions, there was no reason to expect any progress.

On November 29, Hirohito again convened a meeting of the eight former prime ministers: Wakatsuki, Okada, Hirota, Hayashi, Konoe, Hiranuma, Abe, and Yonai. For about an hour they expressed their views on the issues the emperor had raised. Not one of them favored war. Two of the elder statesmen seemed relatively inclined in that direction, while five were firmly opposed. One man stood in between.

Admiral Yonai issued a stern warning: "Forgive me for putting it in colloquial terms, but we must be careful not to jump out of the frying pan and into the fire."

For some reason both Hirohito and Kido remained silent throughout the meeting.

Given America's negative response on the twenty-seventh to Japan's diplomatic proposals, negotiations had reached an impasse and war now seemed an inevitability. Nevertheless, when Hirohito heard through Prince Taka-matsu that the navy was still of a mind to avoid the conflict, he immediately summoned the navy minister and the navy chief of staff. However, as Kido later reported, "When the emperor questioned them, they answered with conviction, so he told me to have the prime minister proceed as planned." In other words, Hirohito was giving the go-ahead for war. Kido quickly relayed the message to Tōjō by phone. It was November 30, 6:30 P.M.

On December 2, the morning after the imperial conference at which war was finally approved, Admiral Isoroku Yamamoto, commander of the combined fleet, which was already in the North Pacific, sent the coded message to Vice-Admiral Nagumo: "Climb Mt. Niitaka, 1208."

War in the Pacific

Japan's naval task force had secretly left Etorofu in the Kurils on November 26. The attack on Pearl Harbor was set for December 8 (December 7 on Hawaii), and the fleet left early in case war was declared. If hostilities were averted at the last minute, the force could always be recalled. Upon receipt of the radio message "Climb Mt. Niitaka, 1208," the fleet of six aircraft carriers and seventeen cruisers and destroyers set a course for Hawaii and pressed ahead in high spirits. Another thirty submarines were already operating in Hawaiian waters and five of them were carrying special mini-subs on their decks. The mini-subs each had a crew of two, were just twenty-four meters long, and displaced a mere forty-four tons. They had been made especially to penetrate the anti-submarine nets laid around Pearl Harbor.

Since the fleet was sailing north of the forty-fifth parallel, well outside normal shipping lanes, it was able to go undetected. By 6:00 A.M. on the seventh (12 noon EST) they were some 230 nautical miles north of Oahu.

Taking advantage of the moonlight, the first wave of 183 planes took off from the decks of the carriers, followed at 7:15 by another wave of 167 planes. In all, 350 planes carrying 765 men swooped out of the sky over a Pearl Harbor that was still asleep on Sunday morning. It was 7:40 A.M. on December 7, 1941.

Although there was a precedent in Japan's surprise attack on Port Arthur during the Russo-Japanese War, the strike on Pearl Harbor, carried out against the emperor's wishes, was indeed a surprise and, from the United States' perspective, a sneak attack. Due to a delay in its translation, the Foreign Affairs Ministry's statement breaking off negotiations was delivered to the United States more than one hour after the scheduled time of 1:00 P.M. on December 7. When Ambassador Nomura and Special Envoy Kurusu finally appeared before Secretary of State Hull, Pearl Harbor had already been turned into a scene from hell. It came out later that the United States had cracked Japan's naval code some time before, and Hull was just feigning ignorance when Nomura handed him Japan's diplomatic note.

That American forces in Hawaii were not in a state of readiness was also an advantage for the Japanese, and the attack, which came off almost perfectly, was from Japan's standpoint a major success. With the exception of its aircraft carriers, virtually all of the United States Pacific Fleet was at anchor in Pearl Harbor that day. In moments, five of its eight battleships were sunk and the remaining three badly damaged. The attackers also sank ten cruisers and destroyers. In contrast, Japanese losses were almost miraculously light: just twenty-nine planes and five mini-subs. Second Lieutenant Sakamaki, a crew member aboard one of the mini-subs, was captured when his submarine ran aground and he was knocked unconscious. He thus became the first Japanese prisoner-of-war in the Pacific.

Meanwhile, General Yamashita's Twenty-fifth Army launched a surprise attack on the Malay Peninsula. The first troops had landed some forty minutes before the Pearl Harbor strike and had quickly advanced. The same thing happened in Hong Kong. On the morning of the eighth a radio announcement was repeatedly broadcast from imperial headquarters: "Before dawn today, in the western Pacific, the Imperial Army and Navy entered into a state of war with the forces of Great Britain and the United States." Throughout the country, Japanese greeted the news with a mixture of anxiety and excitement.

On the tenth, the two battleships of the British East Asian fleet, the *Prince of Wales* and the *Repulse*, were sunk off Malaya by a squadron of naval bombers. Japan's rapid successes at the beginning of the war seemed to confirm the Japanese view of their country as a divine land protected by the gods. In quick succession "the emperor's invincible army" blew through Hong Kong, Manila, Singapore, Rangoon, and Batavia like wind through dead leaves. So quickly did these capitals fall that Hirohito, his face "beaming like I've never seen before," remarked to Kido, "It's so fast. The war is going almost too well!"

***

However, despite their initial victories, the Japanese soon learned that they were not invincible. On April 18, 1942, the undreamt-of happened: The Japanese mainland was bombed for the first time. Two American aircraft carriers had secretly approached Japan from the east. From them sixteen B-25 bombers took off and attacked Tokyo, Nagoya, and Kobe before eluding their pursuers and landing in China. Casualties were light but the shock was great. At imperial headquarters the head of the navy's information office made fun of Colonel James Doolittle, who had led the raids: "Indeed, he could 'do little,' but I'm sure that next time—if there is a next time—he'll be able to 'do nothing.'"

But barely six months into the war, at the Battle of Midway in June 1942, Japan lost four of its precious aircraft carriers and a heavy cruiser and was already allowing effective control of the seas to slip into the hands of the enemy. The downward slide had begun. Then came Guadalcanal (August 1942), the horrible, hellish battle which ended in Japan's withdrawal. Next, Fleet Commander Admiral Yamamoto died when his plane was shot down over Bougainville Island. There followed a series of fiercely fought but unsuccessful defenses: at such places as the Aleutian island of Attu (May 1943), Saipan (July 1944), Guam (August 1944), and Iwo Jima (March 1945). As defeat piled on defeat with ever-increasing speed, the Japanese military devised, in desperation, kamikaze attacks. They could see no other means to fight than this tragic tactic in which plane and pilot became a missile aimed at the enemy's ships.

Hirohito had signed the declaration of war on December 8, 1941, in spite of his reservations, under pressure from the military. After hostilities began, he felt duty-bound to support the war effort. He put aside his former misgivings and, along with the nation, concentrated on the task of defeating the Allies. After the outbreak of the China war, Hirohito had given up golf; thereafter he also gave up horseback riding. Apart from a visit to the Grand Shrine at Ise and one to the Nasu Detached Palace, Hirohito did not leave Tokyo until the war had ended. He lost seven or eight kilos, as he subsisted on wartime rations. Toward the end of the war, when the news was all bad, he suffered a nervous breakdown. He would forget that he had watered his plants and water them again. He took to pacing up and down his room and railing impotently against the military, to the despair of his aides.

On February 12, 1942, the emperor said to Kido: "Let us not lose any opportunity to end the war. It would not be good for humanity if the war were prolonged and the tragedy spread. If it does go on, the Army will get worse. We have to consider the situation carefully and plan accordingly."

After Guadalcanal, Hirohito said to Prince Higashikuni, "The military underestimated the American Army; their sacrifice was in vain." Two years later, with the fall of Saipan, America's B-29s were able to bomb the Japanese mainland, and this became one of the major causes of defeat. With this ended any hope of Japan winning the war. On July 17, 1944, Hirohito said to Prince Higashikuni, "We lost Saipan because we sent all supplies to Rabaul [in the Solomon Islands], paying little attention to the defense of Saipan. This was a serious mistake on the part of the Navy."

General MacArthur, who earlier in the war had been forced to flee to Australia, had sought to recapture the Philippines in an island-by-island northward push, finally reaching the island of Luzon and Manila in January 1945, and thus fulfilling his famous pledge, "I shall return."

As Japan's forces were gradually pushed back, the enemy finally landed on Okinawa. Women, children, grade-school students—all threw themselves into the battle. Their efforts were heroic but ended in crushing defeat. Over 90,000 Japanese soldiers and 94,000 civilians are thought to have died in the horrific struggle. On its way to Okinawa to provide support with only enough fuel for the one-way trip, the *Yamato,* the world's largest battleship and one of the few ships left in the Japanese navy, was bombarded by U.S. planes and sank in 430 meters of water. Thus did the once-proud imperial navy come to what can only be called an ignominious end. The sinking of the *Yamato* came on April 7, 1945, while Okinawa fell on the following June 23.

On the European front, too, the German army was crumbling. On April 29, shortly before the fall of Berlin, Hitler married his lover, Eva Braun, in the bunker. The next day they committed suicide. On the same day Mussolini and his mistress were lynched by an angry Italian mob. Their corpses were hung from a tree in a Milanese square, and for three days the crowds pelted the bodies with stones and beat them with sticks. Italy had already fallen, and now Germany, too, was crushed. This left Japan as the Allies' only enemy. There was not the slightest chance that Japan could hold out; yet, still the militarists continued to call for resistance to the very end. They urged that every civilian be armed with a bamboo spear and made to fight enemy soldiers one by one on Japanese soil.

Ever since the fall of Saipan, regular air raids over Japan had become a genuine threat, and deliveries from the "Tokyo Express" had, in fact, been going on since

November of 1944, at least on a small scale. Matters soon grew worse. On March 10, 1945, a huge squadron of 279 B-29s rained incendiary bombs on central Tokyo. One million one hundred and sixty thousand were made homeless, and over eighty thousand were killed. In the midst of the raid, Hirohito's eldest daughter, Princess Shigeko, who had been married in the autumn of 1943, went into labor in the palace air raid bunker. And there, after the all-clear signal had been sounded, she gave birth to a son, Prince Nobuhiko, the emperor's first grandchild.

Eight days after this air raid, Hirohito went on a tour of inspection to see the damage. The worst of the destruction had already been cleaned up, but many of the homeless had built makeshift shelters from sheets of corrugated iron. The bombed-out concrete shells of buildings and blackened wooden remnants presented a ghostly scene as far as the eye could see. The devastation reminded Hirohito of the battlefields of World War I he had seen in France and Belgium in his youth, and the sight must have made him feel even keener regret over the Pacific War. He turned to Lord Keeper of the Privy Seal Kido, and said, with a look of deep sorrow on his face, "After the Great Kanto Earthquake, everything was so totally, cleanly burnt and destroyed that one did not feel such a sense of shock. But this is far more tragic. It pains me deeply. Tokyo has become 'scorched earth.' "

Yet, the destruction he saw was only a prelude of things to come. Following an April air raid on northern Tokyo, the bombers struck again in May. On May 24 the Americans sent 562 planes, and on the twenty-fifth another 502. The Japanese air force did not have a single plane to send up against these impressive numbers, and could only stand by and watch as the enemy ran rampant. The raid on the twenty-fifth was especially wide-ranging. The bombers dropped 3,260 tons of incendiary bombs on business and government offices in Ginza and Kojimachi, as well as residential districts in central Tokyo.

In earlier raids, parts of the imperial palace grounds had been bombed, but this time nothing was touched. More than 2,000 members of the Palace Security Police, the Metropolitan Fire Department, the Palace Guard, and the Palace Fire Brigade had been deployed around the grounds to extinguish the ash and bits of burning ember that had been falling like rain. When the all-clear sounded at 1:00 A.M., they dispersed. Then, just five minutes later, a servant discovered that a section of the eaves of the main palace building was smoldering. He immediately alerted the security forces. Unfortunately the fire was on the inside of a corridor, and difficult for firemen to reach. In minutes the area was engulfed in flames. There was no time to fight the blaze, so many risked their lives to save what they could from the palace as flames and ash flew around them.

The main palace, begun in 1884, had taken five years to build. Made of the finest cypress wood, it covered some 190,000 square feet. Brilliantly colored paintings were executed on each ceiling panel, and the chandeliers had been brought in from Europe. On each of the sliding partitions, the best artists in Japan had been commissioned to paint traditional designs of birds and flowers. The whole extravagant thing had cost 4,000,000 yen (approximately 30 billion yen by today's rates), but in no time the fire had raced mercilessly along the corridor from which it started, gutting the main hall and the countless rooms connected to it.

Army engineers, seeing that the blaze would inevitably spread to the imperial apartments in the inner palace, came up with the idea of dynamiting the central corridor in the hope that it would contain the fire, but they could not bring it off. Although they pumped all the water out of the numerous ponds in an effort to put out the inferno, it finally engulfed the inner palace, completely destroying it. Ever since its completion sixty years before, the palace had stood as a symbol of Japan's march into a new age. How many people, from the Meiji era on, had stood on the Nijubashi bridge and looked over with pride at the copper roofs of the palace buildings within? But now, in just two hours, it had been reduced to ash.

The efforts to save it had been truly heroic. Thirty-three fire fighters died in the blaze: sixteen firemen, fourteen soldiers, and three palace security guards. The emperor, however, was safe. Six months earlier, he had moved into the palace library. When the air raid sirens sounded, he had escaped to an underground shelter 100 meters northeast of the library. The shelter was built under a low mound. Its solid walls, between one and one and a half meters thick, protected a number of smaller rooms and a large conference room. This room was subsequently to be used twice for imperial conferences, at the second of which the Japanese government decided to accept the Potsdam Declaration and bring the war to an end.

When fire broke out in the main palace, the news was relayed by phone to the chamberlain on duty in the library. He in turn immediately informed Hirohito: "Apparently

flames have spread across the entire back side of the roof.''
The emperor's face suddenly went tense, and he shouted in
a voice that seemed to well up from deep inside: ''The main
hall has caught fire! The main hall! There is so much there
that was precious to the Meiji Emperor, so many irre-
placeable things. I want that fire put out whatever it
takes.'' He was extremely upset and could not be calmed as
he awaited further news. When the report finally came that
the palace buildings were lost, he looked dejected, but he
quickly composed himself and expressed concern for the
scores of women who served at the palace. ''If the fire has
not spread yet to the ladies' quarters, I want every effort
made to protect those buildings.'' Under direct orders from
the emperor, the army engineers successfully dynamited the
200-meter-long gallery that led from the palace to the ladies'
quarters, thus saving the building from the flames.

That night the wind was not particularly strong, but the
intensity of the blaze whipped up a storm of its own.
Hirohito, who had always been respectful of the Shinto
gods, was worried that the fire might spread to the imperial
sanctuary, which housed the palace shrine, just 200 meters
west of the inner palace. The sacred mirror, its main
treasure, was safely locked in a steel box within a concrete
vault deep underneath the shrine, so there was no need for
concern there. But if the building itself burned, it might be
taken as an omen of Japan's own destruction, and there was
no telling what kind of shock it would be to the Japanese
people. Large numbers of fire fighters stood by ready to
protect the shrine, but fortunately the wind shifted and the
sanctuary was spared.

On the same day the Meiji Shrine was also destroyed by

fire, and the shock to Hirohito, who had revered his grandfather, was tremendous. Japan's most sacred shrine, the Grand Shrine at Ise, had already been partially gutted in an earlier fire bombing raid. This, too, affected Hirohito deeply:

> I probably should have brought the imperial mirror from Ise and the imperial sword from Atsuta here so that I could take care of them myself. But in deciding when to move them, I must act cautiously and take into account the effect it would have on the people's morale. Still, if worse comes to the worse, I feel I have no choice but to guard the sacred objects myself and share with them whatever fate has in store.

❀
"Your Majesty's Counsel"

After laying waste to most of Tokyo, the U.S. Air Force took aim on other cities and towns throughout Japan, reducing much of the country to ruin. Japan had virtually no airplanes to send up against the B-29s. With the imperial navy destroyed, the American fleet sailed unopposed along the coasts of Japan, firing freely on military and industrial targets. Food was becoming increasingly scarce, and domestic transportation was paralyzed. "No food to eat, no place to live" seemed to have replaced the fighting spirit. Taking stock of the situation, the emperor decided the time had come to make peace.

On April 5 an imperial conference of elder statesmen was held to consider the selection of a new cabinet to replace the outgoing Koiso administration. At the meeting Tōjō was forceful in his views. "We are facing warfare on our own soil. I feel that in order to unite the nation and the military in this effort, the next prime minister should be drawn from the Army." His suggestion that General Hata be chosen was met with silence around the room. Their only other possible choice was Kantarō Suzuki, the president of the privy council. But Suzuki was a career sailor. He knew nothing of politics and power, and he doubted his own ability to carry the responsibility that was being placed on him. After all, Japan's survival was at stake.

Hirohito tried to persuade him. "I understand your desire to withdraw yourself from consideration, but there is no one else we can turn to in this grave situation." When Suzuki seemed even more reluctant, the emperor tried again. "We need you. I would like you to reconsider." When Hirohito said, "We need you," Suzuki could hardly continue to refuse. It was almost certainly the first time the emperor had used the expression, and it could only have been directed toward Suzuki, who had gained Hirohito's absolute confidence by serving him for seven years as grand chamberlain. Furthermore, Suzuki's wife had been Hirohito's nanny. The emperor believed that working with Suzuki, with whom he had such close ties, he would be able to bring the war to a quick end. But the militarists were still vigorously calling for continued struggle and imprisoning as traitors or defeatists all those who dared to speak of peace. Under these circumstances, it was a difficult for anyone, emperor or otherwise, to advocate a cessation of hostilities.

With the fall of Okinawa in June 1945, the war was lost. In a last, desperate attempt to assure Russian neutrality, the emperor suggested sending Prince Konoe to the Soviet Union as a special envoy. Hirohito hoped he could persuade the Soviets to act as intermediaries in obtaining peace. For their part, the Russians wanted to drag things out a bit more. Delivered on July 18, their reply to the overture was curt: "There is nothing concrete in the proposals Japan has made. Furthermore, Special Envoy Konoe's mission is not clearly defined. Therefore, it is impossible for us to give any sort of definitive reply."

At the same time the Russians were busy at Yalta, agreeing to enter the war against Japan in exchange for Soviet control over southern Sakhalin and the Kuril Islands. On top of that, eight days later, on July 26, came the Potsdam Declaration, outlining what the United States, England, and China intended to do with Japan after the war. On the twenty-seventh the Japanese foreign affairs ministry intercepted a shortwave radio broadcast of the declaration via San Francisco. It called for the following: (1) the disarmament of Japan's military; (2) the elimination of the authority and power of militaristic elements; (3) the establishment of a democratic government; (4) the Allied occupation of Japan until such time as a democratic, peaceful, accountable government was firmly established; (5) the limitation of Japan's territory to the four main islands of Hokkaido, Honshu, Shikoku, and Kyushu, and the various small islands in their immediate vicinity; and (6) the punishment of war criminals. In addition, the declaration stated that the Allies did not intend to enslave the Japanese race or destroy the Japanese nation. It demanded the unconditional surrender of the Japanese military, but it did not touch at all on the questions of the emperor's status or of sovereignty.

The Allies carefully watched for Japan's reaction, but at a press conference Prime Minister Suzuki dismissed the demands. "I don't think that declaration is of much importance. The government will simply ignore it and continue to fight the war to its end." In fact, privately he was committed to working toward Japan's acceptance of the Potsdam declaration's conditions, but to placate the militarists he was compelled to make hawkish statements in public. Even if he was willing to lead Japan to surrender, as prime minister he apparently felt compelled publicly to advocate the continuation of the war until peace was concluded. Unfortunately the Allies interpreted Suzuki's statement to mean that Japan intended to keep fighting, and on August 6 and 9 the Americans dropped atomic bombs on Hiroshima and Nagasaki.

When Foreign Affairs Minister Shigenori Tōgō came to report the tragedy, the emperor was firm: "Since it has reached the point where such new weaponry is being deployed, we cannot continue this war any further. It is impossible. We no longer have the luxury of waiting for an opportune time to begin negotiations. We must concentrate our efforts on ending the war quickly."

On the ninth, the Soviet Union entered the war against Japan, and its troops swept unchecked into Manchuria. The once-proud Kwantung Army, known for its spirit, had withdrawn south, and Russian advance troops had no trouble seizing control of Manchuria. Many Japanese citizens were killed by the advancing Soviets, and the Japanese soldiers captured in Manchuria were condemned to hard labor under poor conditions for many years after the war.

***

Three years and nine months after the outbreak of war, Japan was facing a hopeless situation, and the time had come to accept defeat. Suzuki convened a conference of all the top war leaders to discuss possible responses to the Potsdam Declaration. Six men were present: Prime Minister Suzuki, Foreign Affairs Minister Tōgō, War Minister Anami, Navy Minister Yonai, Army Chief of Staff Umezu, and Naval Chief of Staff Toyoda. The conference lasted for three hours but ended inconclusively. They did agree on one thing, however; that Japan would only accept the declaration if the emperor's position was guaranteed; in other words, they insisted that the national polity created by the Meiji Constitution be preserved. But beyond that they could not agree, for the war minister and the two chiefs of staff set another three conditions: that no occupation force be stationed in Japan proper; that Japanese forces overseas be repatriated by the Japanese themselves and not be required to surrender to Allied troops; and that Japan try its own war criminals.

Foreign Affairs Minister Tōgō opposed these conditions, arguing that they would never be accepted by the Allies, but the military faction would not budge. They were well aware that the enemy would never swallow these terms, and their real aim was to continue the war. In an effort to find some spark of hope in the bleak situation, War Minister Anami argued that if all 100 million Japanese were to fight to their deaths on the homeland, the casualties inflicted on the enemy would be enormous and would put them in a better position to discuss terms. The two chiefs of staff stood behind him in this view.

In the end, however, the prime minister, foreign affairs minister, and navy minister all remained in favor of unconditional surrender—a position the other three refused to accept—and the meeting adjourned without any progress. After a late lunch Prime Minister Suzuki convened a cabinet meeting to discuss the same issue. But again the war minister's opposition confused the situation, and no conclusion was reached. The meeting lasted six and a half hours— from 2:30 in the afternoon to 10:00 at night, with an hour out for dinner—but ended in a stalemate.

Prime Minister Suzuki and the war and navy ministers had been arguing for nearly twelve hours, since the Supreme Council meeting that had begun at 10:30 that morning. The seventy-eight-year-old Suzuki was reaching the limits of exhaustion, but he rallied himself, and at 11:50 that night he presided over another imperial conference. Including Hiranuma, president of the privy council and a former prime minister himself, seven men descended into the meeting room in the air raid shelter under the imperial library, there to meet with Hirohito.

Before the conference, Suzuki filled the emperor in on the cabinet meeting that had been held earlier. The prime minister recognized that, given the obstinacy of the war minister and the two chiefs of staff, the imperial conference would inevitably end in the same deadlock if he were to conduct it as he normally did. So he switched tactics. After each participant had had his say, Suzuki would rise immediately, turn to the emperor and solicit his opinion. He wondered whether Hirohito would go along.

All day long Hirohito had been impatiently following the progress—or rather the lack thereof—of the Supreme Council session and the cabinet meeting, summoning Kido four times for reports. He realized that there was no other way to resolve the situation but to accept Suzuki's opening and offer his own opinion at the imperial conference.

And so the conference opened, with Suzuki and the emperor ready to execute their secret strategy. First to speak was Foreign Affairs Minister Tōgō. When he reiterated his earlier position that Japan should accept the Potsdam Declaration, War Minister Anami, as before, still called for an all-out war effort on the Japanese homeland. Hiranuma at first seemed to support Tōgō's stand, but then allowed that there might be circumstances in which continuing to fight would be the better course. In the end he did not come down clearly on one side or the other. The two chiefs of staff again fell into line behind the war minister, and the breakdown was, as expected, three to three. And since everyone except Hiranuma seemed set in his opinion, it was impossible to know how things might turn out. At that point Prime Minister Suzuki rose from his seat and approached the emperor. He bowed deeply and said: "It has already been nearly two and a half hours and we have yet to resolve our differences. Since the situation is so serious that it does not permit further delay, one wonders if we might not impose upon Your Majesty—however unprecedented it may be—to bring this meeting to a decision by expressing Your exalted views."

Completely stunned by this turn of events, the other six stared at Suzuki, unable to speak. However, the emperor began to speak as soon as Suzuki had finished, as if he had been waiting his turn. "Very well. I shall give my views. I agree with the foreign minister." His voiced echoed through the room as he continued: "Some speak of a last battle on the homeland, but neither the vital defenses at Kujukurihama nor even the armaments our troops will need are adequate. The production of aircraft has not proceeded as planned. Indeed, none of the military's plans seem to be realized. Does anyone suppose we can win a war under the circumstances? When I think of how my loyal troops will be disarmed and how those responsible for the war will be punished, it is truly difficult for me to bear. But now we must bear the unbearable, endure the unendurable. I think of how the Meiji Emperor must have felt at the time of the Triple Intervention* and it is with tears in my eyes that I find myself agreeing with the foreign minister."

He even went so far as to tell his listeners not to let concern about his person or the imperial household stand in the way of peace. All in the room were moved to tears. Prime Minister Suzuki rose from his chair. "One is humbled by such worthy sentiments. Surely in light of them the decision of this body is clear." His announcement was final, allowing for no further debate. Everyone turned toward the emperor and bowed deeply.

It was 2:20 A.M., August 10, and at last, by Emperor Hirohito's own intervention, the end of the war was at hand—Japan had decided to surrender.

Immediately afterward, the cabinet was reconvened, and except for their condition that the national polity should remain intact, they, too, accepted the terms of the Potsdam Declaration. Later the war minister raised another question, this time regarding the wording of America's reply to Japan's surrender announcement. There were two sticking

*In 1895, France, Russia and Germany forced Japan to return the Liatong Peninsula to China—Author's Note.

points in the American response, which read in part: ". . . the authority of the emperor and the said Japanese government to rule the state shall be placed under the jurisdiction of the Supreme Commander of the Allied Powers. . . . The ultimate form of government of Japan shall . . . be established by the freely expressed will of the Japanese people."

First, the statement insisted on "the freely expressed will of the Japanese people," but did not touch on the issue of whether or not the imperial system would be allowed to continue. The second problem was the remark that "the emperor will be subject to the Supreme Commander of the Allied Forces." Taking these issues in reverse order, in translating the statement for domestic consumption, the Japanese government softened the expression "will be subject to" to "will be placed under the jurisdiction of," but the war minister and the chiefs of staff were unappeased. "This would make Japan a vassal state. We must insist on a clause that specifies that the national polity will not be altered."

Hirohito sought to calm him down by saying, "Don't worry, Anami. We are confident." Regarding the point that Japan's government should be "established by the freely expressed will of the Japanese people," Hirohito did not seem especially perturbed. "Even if the Allies recognize the imperial institution, it will do no good unless the people support the system. It doesn't bother me at all that the people should exercise their free will in such matters."

Nevertheless, Japan's first surrender in its history was still not confirmed, so another imperial conference was called for on August 14. This time several new participants were added, including the head of the bureau for naval affairs of the navy ministry, and the chief secretary for the cabinet, making, with Prime Minister Suzuki, eleven men all together.

Suzuki started the meeting. "I realize it is no small offense to trouble Your Majesty yet again for Your views, but after carefully hearing the opinions of those who oppose surrender, I wish to request once again Your Majesty's counsel." The military faction knew that this would be their last opportunity, and in desperation, even tearfully, they pleaded their case to Hirohito. Anami was particularly emotional and broke down several times as he reiterated his opposition to surrender. The participants sat hushed, and even the emperor from time to time removed his glasses and wiped his eyes. After the war minister's speech, Hirohito looked out over the silent group, then began to speak with firm resolve.

"If no one else wishes to speak at this time, I shall convey my thoughts. I believe that it is impossible to continue the war any longer. . . . Naturally there is some concern over the issue of the national polity; it is my belief that the other side has shown appropriate good will in this matter, and I do not think we should doubt them. . . . No matter what may happen to me, I wish to save the lives of my people. At this time I shall do anything that is required of me. I will stand before the microphone at any time. The shock to our troops will doubtless be great, but with the help of the ministers of war and the navy, I hope matters can be kept under control."

As Hirohito spoke earnestly, the others listened, weeping quietly. When he said "No matter what may happen to me . . ." his voice faltered, and he lowered his head for a moment. The weeping in the room turned to louder lamentations, and even the emperor's clear voice, sharp as a knife, was all but drowned out by the noise. The end of the war was, at last, finally assured.

***

After 11:00 that evening, in a room on the palace grounds, Hirohito recorded the imperial rescript announcing Japan's surrender. He began, "After pondering deeply on the circumstances in the world at large, and the conditions that prevail in Our empire, and wishing, through extraordinary measures, to take control of the situation, We are here to report to you, Our good and loyal subjects. . . ."

Exhausted by several sleepless night in a row, he stumbled here and there. After listening to the completed recording, he was dissatisfied. "It didn't go well. I seemed a little too quiet. Let's try it again."

The second time around, his voice was louder, but he made some mistakes in the reading, leaving out one or two conjunctions. There was talk of trying yet again, but they decided not to. Chamberlain Tokugawa locked the record in his office safe until the next morning, when it was handed over to NHK, the official broadcasting service.

Meanwhile, right after the recording session, at about 11:30 P.M., when some of the people involved were leaving the palace, their car was surrounded by an excited mob of soldiers, who took them prisoner and forced them back to the imperial guards' headquarters. Some of the Konoe palace guards had rebelled. Having heard about the recording, two young officers from the war ministry, Major Hatanaka and Lieutenant Colonel Shiizaki, conspired with Majors Koga and Ishihara of the Konoe guards to prevent the emperor's broadcast from going out the next day.

When Takeshi Mori, the commander of the Konoe guards, upbraided them for their disloyalty, they shot him. They then searched through the palace offices from top to bottom, but did not find the recording. The rebels even beat Chamberlain Tokugawa when he refused to cooperate.

Finally word of the incident reached General Seiichi Tanaka, Commander of the Eastern Army, who rushed to the rescue and severely reprimanded the rebels. Earlier, the plotters had tried to subvert soldiers from the Eastern Army and the Konoe palace guards to join them, but their efforts had been wasted. It was clear to them now that their plan had failed, so they complied with Tanaka's order to surrender.

Major Koga, who was Tōjō's son-in-law, committed suicide in front of the corpse of his dead commander. Those who had known him, without exception, were effusive in their praise for his character. Shiizaki and Hatanaka chose to shoot themselves, and by next morning's light the palace uprising, which had threatened the emperor himself, had been put down.

As for Hirohito, he had just fallen asleep after finishing the recording when he was awakened with the news of the rebellion. One may well imagine that, as was his habit at such times, he must have spent most of the night uncomfortably in the throne room, pacing back and forth, talking to himself. Toward daybreak he lamented to Grand

Chamberlain Hisanori Fujita, "What on earth do these men have in mind? Why do they not understand how much this pains me?"

Shortly thereafter, when Commander Tanaka arrived at the imperial library, Hirohito praised him for his services in quelling the insurrection, but some days later Tanaka took his own life, feeling that he bore ultimate responsibility in the matter. War Minister Anami, too, at the height of the rebellion, killed himself at home, hoping that his "death would atone for his crime."

The road to surrender was long and difficult, but August 15 arrived at last.

PART THREE:

THE EMPEROR'S PEACE

Another Emperor Outside
the Moat

Prime Minister Suzuki resigned on the day of Japan's unconditional surrender. In an unprecedented move Prince Naruhiko Higashikuni, a member of the imperial family, was named to succeed him. In his younger days, the prince, after a quarrel with his brother-in-law, Emperor Taishō, had left Japan and spent many stormy years in France. But now he was a general in the army and quite settled. As father-in-law to the emperor's daughter Princess Teru, he was very close to Hirohito.

Ever since the Meiji era, members of the imperial family had been forbidden from engaging in political activities for fear that such involvement might adversely affect the emperor. But Japan had never lost a war before. It seemed a good idea to permit an exception in this case and make temporary use of imperial prestige in order to help the nation ride out the crisis.

And there was a mountain of problems to face. First, the government had to put down unrest among those in the military who opposed the surrender, such as the rebels of the Atsugi Air Corps. And of course they needed to prepare for the arrival of the Occupation troops. Japan's overseas forces (the Kwantung Army, the China Expeditionary Army, and the Southern Army) had to be given the emperor's surrender order, disarmed, and then repatriated. And then there were the measures demanded by the Potsdam Declaration: the maintenance of public order; the dissolution of the army and navy, and the demobilization of all military personnel; the investigation of war crimes; and the disbanding of the thought police. Beyond all that, of course, loomed the need to rebuild the economy and establish a blueprint for a peaceful Japan.

All these problems were pressing in the extreme. Japan faced a difficult, fearful road, and its leaders were apprehensive. Yet, the nation was surprisingly calm. To have a prime minister who, as a member of the imperial family, could call upon the prestige of the emperor would go a long way toward providing the kind of drive necessary to get things done. And it should not be forgotten that, after fifteen years of continuous war, the Japanese people had no more stomach for conflict. Indeed, they had been battered so completely during those years that they were now overwhelmed with a feeling of powerlessness.

On August 28 the first detachment of American troops flew in, followed two days later by MacArthur. Holding his corncob pipe, he bellowed proudly as he descended from the plane, "The road to Tokyo has been long." He was greeted with impassive stares from the Japanese. American army and navy units began landing one after the other at Yokohama and Yokosuka, then spread out across the country. The U.S. Pacific Fleet anchored in Tokyo Bay, and on

September 2 the formal signing of the surrender document took place on the deck of the battleship *Missouri*. Japan's chief delegate was former foreign affairs minister Mamoru Shigemitsu, who had lost his leg in a terrorist bombing in Shanghai in 1932. The sight of Shigemitsu painfully dragging his wooden leg was a tragic reminder of Japan's own ruinous defeat.

From his temporary lodgings at Yokohama's New Grand Hotel, MacArthur moved into the American ambassador's Tokyo residence on September 8. On the seventeenth, the Allied Powers General Command Headquarters (GHQ) was set up in the the Daiichi Mutual Life Insurance Building across the moat from the ruins of the imperial palace. MacArthur's stated intention had been to reduce Japan to the status of a fourth-rate power, but to Japan's good fortune the initial plan to impose a military government on the nation had been scrapped, and instead the decision was made to leave the Japanese government intact. The decision was originally intended to make the Occupation run more smoothly, but the effect was to leave Japan with at least some measure of self-government. That being said, the Occupation authorities still held the knife of potential vengeance at Japan's throat, and as if to remind people of where the real power lay, one of GHQ's first acts, on September 11, was to arrest Tōjō and thirty-eight others as war criminals and incarcerate them in Sugamo Prison.

During the war General Tōjō had been the one to proclaim the battlefield rule "Do not accept the disgrace of being captured alive." And now with troops surrounding his house to arrest him, he attempted to commit suicide by shooting himself in the heart. Fortunately or unfortunately, as he pulled the trigger his hand jerked, causing his aim to go off just a fraction. The bullet passed through his lung, missing his heart by a centimeter. The injury was nearly fatal. But much to the surprise of the Japanese, given his designation as a war criminal, Tōjō was rushed to a U.S. army field hospital in Yokohama. Arrests of war criminals continued apace. Important people from all walks of life— the military, politics, the government, finance, and the arts—waited apprehensively.

Hirohito himself was beset with worries. He said to Kido, "It is most painful to hand over as war criminals those whom until just yesterday I relied upon as my right-hand men. It is an unbearable position to be in. Is it impossible to think that I might accept all the responsibility myself and abdicate?" Kido was opposed to the idea. "Were Your Majesty to retire now, it would shake the very foundations of the imperial institution."

Undoubtedly the emperor was deeply upset at the arrest of many of his aides, yet he himself was in a precarious position, not knowing what fate had in store for him. Would the Americans arrest him as a war criminal? Would they demand that he abdicate? GHQ gave no indication at all of its plans, and there was no way of guessing what they were thinking. General MacArthur could afford to sit back, as if waiting for a beast to fall into his trap. As the general recalled later, to summon Hirohito "would be to outrage the feelings of the Japanese people and make a martyr of the emperor in their eyes. No, I shall wait, and in time the emperor will voluntarily come to see me."

Not knowing that MacArthur was thinking along the very same lines, the Imperial Household Ministry sent

Grand Chamberlain Fujita as Hirohito's emissary to the general's headquarters. Although he arrived at the appointed time, Fujita was kept waiting in the lobby for quite some time and was told the general was meeting with someone else at the moment. The chamberlain was disturbed that the emperor's representative should be treated in this manner. When he was finally ushered into the MacArthur's office, the general was there alone, waiting for him. Fujita spoke first, on behalf of the emperor. "General, since the beginning of the war, you have fought on many different battlefields. How is your health? The sweltering temperatures of the South Pacific can take their toll. And of course Japan's own late summer heat is quite severe. One hopes that you are taking good care of yourself."

MacArthur answered politely, "I am moved by your concern for my well-being. Please convey my regards to His Majesty." But the discussion went no further than that.

Later, Foreign Affairs Minister Shigeru Yoshida met with MacArthur to learn more and to broach an idea. "The emperor wishes to visit Your Excellency." MacArthur replied, "That our occupation of Japan has gone so smoothly is due in large part, I believe, to the emperor's cooperation. I would be delighted if he were to pay me a call." And so arrangements were made for Hirohito to come to the American Embassy on September 27 at 10:00 A.M.

***

On the appointed day the emperor and an unusually small retinue of four cars set out from the imperial palace.

According to notes kept by Motohiko Kakei of the Imperial Household Ministry, Hirohito was "wearing an extremely somber expression" as he left the building, and those who had come to see him off, including the empress and various aides, also "looked very stiff."

As the modest motorcade reached the street, there were no police officers to stop the traffic. MacArthur had ordered no guards for the procession, and a minimum of attendants. Furthermore, the general had let it be known that he would not meet Hirohito at the entrance of the embassy, but would greet him inside, in the hallway by the entrance to the room where they were to talk. This was in sharp contrast to the practices that had prevailed before Japan's defeat. When the emperor left the palace then, the police would stop all traffic thirty minutes before his departure, and an advance guard of motorcycles would speed along ahead, clearing everyone from the route. How keenly must his retinue now felt the truism that all is change in this world.

Just as the motorcade reached the Toranomon crossroad, the traffic signal turned red, and the emperor's car came to a stop like everyone else's. The chamberlain accompanying the emperor reported that a passenger on a tram that had stopped next the emperor's car stared at them with a puzzled look on his face, as if he were trying to work out why the emperor's motorcade had come to a halt.

When they arrived at MacArthur's residence, within the American Embassy compound, the American aides lined up at the entrance stared coldly at Hirohito. As he got out of the car he looked bewildered and lost. Suddenly, Brigadier General Bonner Fellers stepped forward, stuck out his hand, and said with a smile, "Welcome, sir!" Hirohito was apparently very moved by the gesture. Upon returning to the palace he asked: "Who was that friendly man who shook my hand?" After finding out his name, he sent the general his photograph, signed "Hirohito" in English. General Fellers was a cousin to Gwen Terasaki, the American wife of Hidenari Terasaki, a counselor in the foreign affairs ministry, later a member of the Imperial Household staff, and an interpreter at the meetings between Hirohito and MacArthur.

The meeting took place in a hall on the second floor. An unsmiling MacArthur met the emperor at the door just outside the room and gave him a very businesslike handshake. He was living up to his American nickname, "Granite Face." An army photographer was ready and waiting, and took three photographs of the two men. There stood the general, over six feet tall, dressed casually, without even a necktie, hands on hips, standing at ease with his legs apart. Next to him was the five foot three Hirohito, proper and stiff in his morning coat. The following day the photograph was carried on the front page of every newspaper in the country. The shock was like a hammer blow to the Japanese. It conveyed better than a thousand words the reality of Japan's defeat and the new, subordinate position their "living god," the emperor, now held in relation to MacArthur.

In the hall where they met, a thick, soft carpet lay on the floor. MacArthur and Hirohito sat on either side of a table next to the fireplace while the interpreter, Katsuzō Okumura, sat at between them. The Imperial Household minister, the grand chamberlain, and the three others in

Hirohito's party were shown into another room. During the meeting a Japanese employee of the embassy brought coffee, but the emperor was too nervous to drink it. In fact, apparently Hirohito was so tense that day that he was trembling much of the time. Yet, there is also the possibility that he did not touch the coffee because of a fear of being poisoned. It seems that his aides had advised him not to eat or drink anything that was offered to him. In fact, when it was decided that Hirohito would pay a call on MacArthur, some members of the Imperial Household worried whether he would be safe visiting the American Embassy. Voices questioning the emperor's role in and his responsibility for the war were getting louder, and furthermore Tōjō had just been arrested. Hirohito himself wondered if something might happen to him.

Hirohito's aides grew more and more anxious as the meeting ran over schedule. Ten minutes after it was supposed to have ended, they heard two voices in the hallway. Hirohito and MacArthur appeared with happy looks on their faces. The general's expression had warmed considerably in forty minutes, and the emperor's usually tranquil look had returned. Then, after Hirohito introduced his aides to MacArthur, the latter saw them all the way back to their cars at the entrance. MacArthur, who had vowed beforehand not to see them off at the entrance, was now breaking his own word, and the change in his attitude toward Hirohito was visible. Perhaps the general caught himself and feared he had given too much away, because he did not, after all, shake Hirohito's hand before the latter got into his car, nor did he wait for the car to leave. Rather, he quickly turned on his heels and went back inside. For his

Hirohito at eight months

In the uniform of an army lieutenant

General Maresuke Nogi

Count Sumiyoshi Kawamura

Hirohito (center) and his classmates at the Peers' School

In British uniform during his state
visit to London

Taking the salute as regent

In his laboratory in the Akasaka Detached Palace

The imperial couple with their first child, Princess
Teru Shigeko, who was born in 1926

In coronation robes

Welcoming Pu Yi, emperor of Manchukuo

Inspecting the damage after an air raid in March 1945

With General MacArthur on September 27, 1945

Visiting a coal mine in 1947

Inspecting marine specimens with Crown Prince Akihito in 1952

With Vice-President and Mrs. Bush during their visit to Japan in 1982

Hirohito's state funeral, held in Tokyo on February 24, 1989

part Hirohito could hardly conceal his happiness in the car on the way back to the palace. He was much more talkative than usual with his chamberlain.

It was indeed to Japan's great good fortune that Mac-Arthur took a liking to the emperor, but what had happened to change the general's mind? The interpreter, Okumura, had made notes during the meeting. One copy went to the Foreign Affairs Ministry and the other, contrary to normal procedure, went into Hirohito's personal files. MacArthur and Hirohito had agreed to keep the proceedings of their talk secret, but years later MacArthur told his side of the story in his memoirs. And in December 1975, the magazine *Bungei Shunjū* published the contents of Okumura's notes. However, in Okumura's account there is no mention of Hirohito offering to take "sole responsibility" for the war. There is other evidence to work from. In an article in the September 14, 1955, edition of the *Yomiuri Newspaper,* former foreign minister Shigemitsu recounted the story he had heard from MacArthur himself when he visited the general in the United States. The general quoted the emperor as follows:

> I bear sole responsibility for whatever happened, for whatever incidents occurred in conjunction with Japan's prosecution of the war. Furthermore, I bear direct and sole responsibility for every action taken in Japan's name by every commander, every soldier, and every politician. As for my own life, whatever judgment you choose to make, it does not matter to me. I bear sole responsibility.

It is hard to believe that Okumura would have left

147

something like this out of his account. But it is also hard to believe that General MacArthur would have invented it. Given Emperor Hirohito's personality, one is inclined to believe MacArthur's story; yet, some doubt still remains as to what really happened.

Friends and Enemies

The arrests of war criminals picked up momentum after Tōjō's detention until the unimaginable finally happened: They reached into the imperial family itself. From December some of Hirohito's top aides, including Lord Keeper of the Privy Seal Kido, his closest confidant, received notification of their pending arrests. Prince Fumimaro Konoe was also among them. Just one month earlier the prince had been asked by MacArthur to take part in drafting the new constitution. Then, just as he was sure he had nothing to fear, his commission was rescinded and replaced by an arrest warrant. Only days before, the proud Konoe had asked Prince Morimasa Nashimoto, upon hearing of the latter's pending arrest, "Why didn't you kill yourself?" It was clear that he himself would not put up with the humiliation of being detained. The night before he was to be taken into custody he committed suicide by swallowing cyanide. This tragic figure, who as prime minister had been drawn despite himself into league with the militarists, was only fifty-four when he died. His funeral was held in a cold, early-winter drizzle; only about 400 people attended. His old friends were afraid they might be condemned as collaborators by the Occupation authorities. The same thing had happened when Prince Nashimoto was arrested—only his daughter was there to see him off; other members of the imperial family stayed away.

While so many of those who had until now been influential and powerful were being thrown in jail, another group was tasting freedom again after many years. The Occupation authorities ordered the release of nearly 3,000 political prisoners, most of them members of the banned Japan Communist party. Once free, Kyū-ichi Tokuda, Yoshio Shiga, and others, who had refused to renounce communism during their eighteen years in prison, held a public meeting to discuss the pursuit of war criminals. They drew up a list of 1,600 accused war criminals, headed by the emperor and the rest of the imperial family. They called for Hirohito's prosecution, for the disestablishment of the imperial system, and the formation of a democratic people's government. Up until barely three months before, no Japanese would have dreamt of criticizing the emperor in public, and while they recognized that it was now a different world, many were put off by the ferocity of the Communist party's attacks.

In January 1946 another well-known Communist, Sanzō Nosaka, who had spent many years in China in antimilitarist activities, returned to Japan to a hero's welcome. Once branded as a traitor, Nosaka was now being hailed as the nation's savior. With his outgoing personality and his gentlemanly speech and manner, he helped turn the Communist party image around. Once feared, the Communists were now gaining popular support.

The Communists gave vent most openly to their anti-imperial sentiments in a magazine called *Shinsō* (*Fact*), which reported scandals among politicians, the military and royals alike. Its attacks on the emperor and empress were especially merciless, causing some people to feel that perhaps the move toward democratization had gone a little too far.

***

From this point onward, GHQ began putting forward its plans for sweeping reforms in several areas of government. Prince Higashikuni's cabinet was less than enthusiastic about the reforms, and his opposition drew the disapproval of the Occupation authorities. On October 4, tired of foot-dragging on the part of the government, GHQ issued several sweeping directives, among them the release of all political prisoners; the dismissal of Home Minister Iwao Yamazaki; the disbanding of the "thought police" and the dismissal of the head of the security forces; and the revocation of all laws limiting the civil rights of citizens. It was clear evidence of GHQ's lack of confidence in the government, and Prince Higashikuni's entire cabinet immediately resigned after only fifty days in office. In appraising the role of the Higashikuni cabinet, we must keep in mind that it was precisely because it drew on the prestige of the imperial family that Japan was able to ride out the uncertainties of defeat without major social disruption.

When it came to naming the next prime minister, Kido

and others privately suggested either Kijūrō Shidehara or Foreign Affairs Minister Shigeru Yoshida. The emperor agreed. Yoshida arranged a meeting with Richard Sutherland, MacArthur's chief of staff, and forcefully recommended Shidehara for the post. MacArthur, who had joined the meeting, said, "GHQ has no intention of interfering in Japan's domestic politics. Judging from what I've just heard about his background, I think Shidehara is someone I would like."

Thus Shidehara, who had been roundly criticized by the rightists for his "soft and weak" approach to foreign policy when he was foreign minister in the 1920s, became Japan's second postwar premier. As a longstanding believer in democracy, and with the reputation of being pro-British and pro-American, he was an excellent choice to be premier under the Occupation. Among other things, the Shidehara cabinet presided over the dissolution of the Japanese armed forces. The first stage—the demobilization of the troops and the dismantling of the military establishment—which had been under way since August, was now complete. Then, on November 30 both the war and navy ministries were abolished, ringing down the final curtain on the once proud imperial armed forces. Many Japanese had lived all their lives with the victories and defeats of the imperial army and navy, through the Sino-Japanese and Russo-Japanese Wars, through World War I, Manchuria, China, and finally the Pacific War. They were saddened by the inglorious end of the military whose traditions stretched back more than seventy years to Emperor Meiji's reign.

From this day, too, the emperor stopped wearing his usual army uniform. Instead he donned an outfit inspired by a naval officer's uniform, which was dubbed "the emperor's uniform." It had a chrysanthemum-leaf pattern embroidered on the collar and at the cuffs, and the imperial chrysanthemum crest on the cap. On November 12, when he wore it for the first time outside Tokyo, on a trip to the Grand Shrine at Ise to report to the sun goddess that the war had ended, the "uniform" was widely criticized. People felt that in the new era of peace a civilian suit would be more appropriate. They pointed out that European royals now wore suits when they went out in public, and they maintained that the Imperial Household Ministry was not showing very good sense when it purposely had the emperor wear a formal uniform that was so clearly patterned after military wear. When Hirohito wore the uniform at the opening ceremonies of the Diet, it again drew criticism. At this point the Imperial Household Ministry began to lose confidence in the idea and abandoned the uniform. Henceforth, the emperor would wear suits or a morning coat. If it had only been a matter of pleasing the general public, the ministry would probably have just ignored the criticism, but they were afraid that the debate might give a bad impression to GHQ, something they wanted to avoid at all costs.

* * *

With Japan's defeat, the imperial palace began to slip into disrepair and untidiness. It was just then, to the great surprise and joy of the palace maintenance staff, that a volunteer group was formed to help with the upkeep of the grounds. A group of villagers from Kurihara County in

Miyagi Prefecture (about 150 miles north of Tokyo), hearing that the plaza in front of the palace had been overrun by weeds, offered to clean it up. It occurred to the Imperial Household Ministry that these volunteers might also be asked to work on the main palace grounds, which still bore the scars of air raid fires. The worst of the damage from the May air raids had been cleared, but because of the chaos surrounding the end of the war and the cutbacks in palace personnel ordered by GHQ, most of the rubble still lay in the heaps into which it had hastily been swept. When the volunteers heard that their help was needed in parts of the grounds previously closed to the public, it was their turn to rejoice. They returned home and recruited people from over sixty villages. The volunteers crammed into trains, carrying their provisions on their backs, for the ride to Tokyo. The bulk of the group—men and women from farming families—arrived on December 8. They marched into the palace through the Sakashita Gate, turned left, and started up the gentle slope. Suddenly they fell silent. Of course, they knew beforehand that all that was left of the once grand palace was stacks of tiles, but now, there in front of them, were the actual pitiful ruins: red, twisted metal skeletons, objects that had been burnt, scorched, and melted into unrecognizable lumps, and, scattered among the dried grass, roof tiles stamped with the chrysanthemum crest. As the volunteers surveyed the scene without a word, P-38 fighter planes buzzed noisily overhead. December 8 was the anniversary of the start of the Pacific War, and, as the volunteers later learned, the Occupation authorities, concerned that there might be incidents, were strictly patrolling the palace area.

In the chill wind the volunteers picked up broken tiles, metal shards, and bits of concrete, and tossed them into large baskets, which they emptied inside an area that had been walled off with stacks of burnt tiles. Hard at work, they paid little attention to a group of people walking toward the site until their leader suddenly realized that the emperor was among them. The volunteers had not recognized Hirohito because he was not dressed in the military uniform he always wore when photographed, but in a brown suit and a soft-brimmed hat. He had heard of their efforts and was touched. Watching them through the window of the palace maintenance offices, he had decided to go and thank them in person. "I should like to meet these people. Please make the necessary arrangements," he had ordered. Chamberlain Kinoshita, although taken aback by the unusual request, had hurried off to where the volunteers were working.

Hirohito arrived, looking frail and trembling, according to accounts given later by those present. He thanked the volunteers for their efforts, then asked them about their trip and life back home. He also inquired about the conditions faced by the demobilized soldiers in the villages and about fertilizer and crops. The scene recalled Japan's mythical "Golden Age," when legend had it that the emperor and his subjects had interacted freely. As Hirohito turned to leave, some of the volunteers began to sing the national anthem, even though it had been banned by GHQ. The emperor paused to listen, and the workers, overcome by emotion, could not finish the song. When he got back to the palace maintenance office, Hirohito telephoned the empress and urged her to visit the workers, too. Later that afternoon she went to the work site and made it a point to talk with the women volunteers.

These "sweeping brigades" from northeastern Honshu have lasted for more than forty years. During this period nearly one million people have participated. For three or four days every year they come to pull weeds and pick up dead leaves in the palace grounds. On another day they help out at the crown prince's palace. In return they are personally greeted and thanked by the imperial couple and the crown prince. They also get a tour of the inner palace, and when they leave they receive ten cigarettes and two small cakes imprinted with the imperial crest. There is never a shortage of applicants.

**

Our great Lord
Since he is a god,
He makes his home
Above the clouds of Heaven
And their attendant thunder.

Kakinomoto-no-Hitomaro (A.D. 690–710)
(from the Man'yōshū)

According to the *Kojiki* and the *Nihon Shoki,* Japan's earliest written records, the emperors have been revered as "living gods" since ancient times. This veneration of the aristocracy and reverence for the imperial house has been passed from generation to generation. Even in medieval times, when the warrior class rose to power and the imperial court and the aristocracy all but disappeared, a deep-rooted respect for the imperial institution remained in the people.

From the Meiji period onward the Imperial Japanese Constitution gave legal weight to the emperor's divine origins. He was called "a god in this world," or "a god in human form," and as these expressions imply, he was seen as a kind of superhuman being who lived "above the clouds." The separation of the emperor from his subjects reached even greater extremes in the Shōwa era. With the rise of the military, the emperor was exalted as an absolute ruler, and his prestige was used to justify the army's dreams of conquest.

On August 15, 1945, the emperor's image of absolute authority faded into history. The Occupation authorities, too, were determined to tear away the imperial house's veil of divinity. At the beginning of October, GHQ ordered the disestablishment of State Shinto and forbade the imperial family from patronizing the cult.

Shortly thereafter they published the value of the assets of the imperial family: 1,590,000,000 yen. People were amazed to learn that this astronomical figure placed the family as the world's wealthiest. Twenty days later these assets were frozen, and from that day on the imperial household budget required the approval of GHQ. In fact, GHQ bluntly stated in a directive, "The Japanese government must act . . . to demystify the imperial family." But Brigadier General Dyke, the head of the Civil Information and Education Bureau, felt that the government was dragging its feet over the matter, so he came up with the sort of plan a military man might devise: He attempted to outflank his adversaries. Through Reginald Bryce, a teacher at the prestigious Peers' School and a longtime friend of Japan, he let it be known that GHQ would like the emperor, on his

157

own and without any direct orders from SCAP, to renounce his divinity. Bryce spoke to the school principal, who passed the message to the Imperial Household minister, who then conveyed it to Hirohito.

Up till then Hirohito was at the center of a stormy controversy. Was he a war criminal? Should he abdicate? Was he to be tried and executed? He himself was searching for a way to redefine himself in the new era that Japan faced. He immediately agreed to the suggestion, as did Prime Minister Shidehara, who saw it as just the right move. For years the target of attacks by militarists and right-wingers for his pro-Western sympathies, Shidehara saw the concept of a divine emperor as not only antiquated but also as the cause of great suffering. The prime minister began drafting the announcement in English. He chose English because the imperial rescript he was preparing was more for the consumption of the GHQ and foreign countries than for the Japanese themselves. On top of that, he actually felt more comfortable writing in English than in Japanese.

On December 28 he showed the finished draft to Hirohito, who nodded his approval, saying it was "just fine," though he wanted added as a preface a reference to Emperor Meiji's Charter Oath of Five Articles, which had set the guidelines for the Japanese state in 1868. The completed rescript was published and broadcast on January 1, 1946, and has come to be known as "The Emperor's Proclamation of His Humanity." It reads, in part: ". . . The ties between Us and Our people have always stood upon mutual trust and affection. They do not depend upon mere legends and myths. They are not predicated on the false conception that the emperor is divine, and that the Japanese people are superior to other races and fated to rule the world.''

Hirohito's renunciation of his divinity struck the Japanese people like a thunderbolt, and they were deeply impressed by the break with tradition it represented. As an epoch-making step, it also drew high marks from GHQ and overseas.

***

Hirohito, still pained by his responsibility for Japan's defeat, felt that perhaps he could do a kind of penance by taking a tour around Japan, a pilgrimage of sorts. For someone like Hirohito, who was introverted to begin with and had lived in isolation almost all his life "above the clouds," it took a great deal of courage and determination suddenly to go out into the world and meet his people face-to-face. On top of that, there was reason to fear an assassin's attack, be it by someone among the many who resented the emperor or some left-wing terrorist. But there was no denying the need he felt to go out among his subjects, who had suffered from the ravages of the war and sacrificed their own family members, and to try to comfort them and encourage them as they rebuilt Japan.

In February 1946 he started in Kawasaki City, at the Shōwa Denkō plant, which had been badly damaged by heavy bombing during the war. Unaccustomed as he was to conversation, at each break he would say, "*Ah sō?*" ("Oh, really?''), which quickly became his trademark.

Wherever he went after that, large crowds came out to see him, perhaps out of curiosity as much as anything else. And the emperor they were seeing now, warm of countenance and unaffected in attitude, contrasted sharply with the solemn monarch in military uniform they had seen before. People could hardly believe it. In Osaka, Nagoya, and other cities on his itinerary, crowds of thousands got out of hand and pressed forward to see Hirohito, trapping him in a sea of humanity. Anxious police could only look on in trepidation as he had his feet trampled on, and his buttons torn off. On one such day he said to his chamberlain when they got back to their lodgings for the evening, "The people were really wild again today, weren't they?" His face broke into a smile.

The term "lodgings" is somewhat grand to describe where Hirohito really had to stay. Since virtually no part of Japan had been untouched by the war's devastation, he and his entourage bedded down where they could, sometimes in the formal reception room of the local government office, or in a public hall, an elementary-school classroom, or even in a railroad car stopped for the night on a railroad siding. The chamberlain worried about how Hirohito might bathe, but the emperor himself was unconcerned. "I can go ten days without bathing. It doesn't matter," he insisted.

Even in the palace he was in the habit of bathing only once every two or three days, and always a very quick bath at that. While he was in Shikoku his relatively infrequent bathing made for an amusing incident. A certain innkeeper in the town of Uwajima, honored that the emperor was planning to stay at his inn, spent a great deal of money refurbishing the baths in his establishment. He waited with anticipation for the imperial visit, but was disappointed when Hirohito arrived and went straight to bed without bathing.

Two of the emperor's doctors decided to use the bath in his place, thinking it a waste not to use the water that had been heated up for the occasion. But once they got in, they noticed that the water was draining rapidly, and before long they had to get out. It seems that the innkeeper, disappointed that the emperor was not going to use the bath, pulled the plug when he found two mere court doctors in the water. There was another reason for the innkeeper's anger: After the emperor finished the bath he was supposed to have taken, the innkeeper had promised local dignitaries that they could then bathe in the same water. And to the innkeeper's dismay, there they were, all lined up in their morning coats, awaiting their turn.

The emperor's travels through Japan yielded any number of anecdotes. Once, for example, he marveled at the practicality of an inn. "These inns are really designed so that it is easy for people to stay in them." Hirohito was prepared to bear many inconveniences and hardships. Once he visited a coal mine 500 meters underground to thank the miners for their work. To greet people in remote farming and fishing villages, he would tramp along the paths between rice fields, and visit fishermen off-loading their catch.

Since time and again he disingenuously lifted his soft-brimmed hat in salutation, by the end of each day it would lose its shape, and each evening it fell to his young page or chamberlain to straighten it out again.

One side effect of the emperor's trip was that GHQ and the Allied Forces were compelled once again to recognize just how popular he was among his people, in contrast to other leaders of countries that had lost a war. Hitler, of course, had killed himself, and Mussolini had been lynched and left to hang for three days. King Victor Emmanuel of Italy had fled the country, and although his eldest son took the throne, after a month he, too, was forced to flee. And there was King Leopold III of Belgium. Belgium had been occupied by Germany, and after the war its people could not forgive Leopold for collaborating with the Nazis. When he tried to return to rule the country in 1950, he was forced to abdicate in favor of his son. In contrast to these pitiful stories, which were still fresh in people's minds, here was the emperor receiving the warmest of receptions as he traveled throughout Japan. To the Japanese it was not all that strange. But one British newspaper wrote with surprise: "Japan has lost the war and is now occupied by foreign troops, but the emperor's popularity has scarcely waned. As he traveled throughout the country, the emperor was greeted by large crowds as if he were some sort of superman. In Japanese society, so thoroughly destroyed in the war, the emperor is the one point of stability."

For its part, one of the reasons GHQ had permitted Hirohito's trip was that they hoped it would serve as a barometer of public feelings toward him. By the degree of popular approval shown to the emperor, the Occupation authorities could better plan how to handle Hirohito and how to approach the upcoming International Military Tribunal for the Far East. Led by the Soviet Union, one faction among the Allies had been demanding that the emperor be arrested and tried as a war criminal, but GHQ recognized how valuable he could be in carrying out their policies. Reflecting on the effects of the trip, MacArthur said, "Having the emperor around is as good as twenty divisions of U.S. troops."

162

But not everyone in Japan saw this trip the same way. The emperor had outspoken critics, especially in the Communist party. At first they took the rather cool stance that no matter how hard Hirohito tried to win public affection, he would only alienate people, and invite their scorn. But gradually they became more emotional: "Although the emperor is more responsible than anyone else for Japan's war of aggression, he has recently embarked on a national tour, addressing people along the way, in an effort to make us forget his responsibility. His actions, clearly on behalf of the reactionary parties in the upcoming elections, are nothing more than an attempt to raise support for the imperial system and set back democratization in Japan." They even ridiculed him, calling him "the Imperial Broom," because wherever he went the streets and towns were cleaned up in preparation for his visit.

Riding Out the Storm

With the Occupation, Japan's existing institutions faced constant attacks from GHQ, but on the most fundamental issue, the imperial system, the authorities maintained a guarded silence. Keeping a careful eye on attitudes both domestic and foreign, they seemed to be keeping the matter as a kind of trump card.

Judging from overseas reactions, many among the Allies were inclined to view the question harshly:

> Japan should abolish the imperial system and reorganize itself. The irrational mythology surrounding the origins of the emperor should also be abolished. [A United States senator]

> In Japan, let at least twenty years pass without anyone as emperor. During that time, re-educate the people to democracy, tear down the mythology surrounding the emperor, then let the people decide by ballot whether they want a republic or a constitutional monarchy. [An American newspaper]

164

Let us abolish the imperial system immediately, and try the emperor and the imperial family as war criminals. [A Soviet broadcast]

China should pronounce sentence on the emperor as a war criminal. [A Chinese parliamentary resolution]

The abolitionists were headed by China and included the Soviet Union, Australia, New Zealand, and the Philippines. England, itself a monarchy, gave passive support to the imperial institution, perhaps because so many former monarchies had become republics, and the British did not want to see the system undermined further. In the United States, Secretary of State Joseph Grew, a former ambassador to Japan, maintained, "Like the Pope and Catholicism, the emperor's existence is essential to Japan; thus the country should democratize while holding on to the imperial system."

Likewise, former British ambassador to Japan Sir Robert Craigie told his countrymen: "If one suddenly abolishes the imperial system, which has a very long history, Japan will fall into chaos, and there is great danger that this will bring about an aggressive, militaristic form of Communism there."

Hirohito, too, was greatly troubled by the question. He brought up the matter with Kido. "One way to handle it would be to go around feigning ignorance, but maybe it would be better to tell some newspaper reporters the whole story [behind the events leading up to the war]. Or perhaps I should talk to MacArthur."

Kido did not agree. He felt that any attempt to explain would be useless and might actually complicate matters. As for MacArthur, at first he favored a republic, but as time passed he began to lean toward maintaining the imperial institution. Part of this was no doubt due to the favorable impression he had of Hirohito after their many meetings. But more than anything, MacArthur wanted his occupation policies to be carried out smoothly, and he wanted to build a lasting monument of sorts to his efforts. He also hoped that a peace treaty could be concluded based on the success of his plans and that, on the strength of that, he could make a run for the United States presidency. In fact, when he returned to the U.S., he did announce his candidacy, but lost out at the convention. In his ambition, he saw that even in defeat the Japanese continued to revere the emperor without question, so he decided to "tame the tiger" rather than kill it.

When Foreign Affairs Minister Shigeru Yoshida came to consult MacArthur on certain public-relations matters, he casually brought up the question of Hirohito's future, hoping to sound MacArthur out. He found the general magnanimous. On November 27, 1945, during a meeting with Navy Minister Yonai, MacArthur said something that convinced the minister that he was not thinking of changing the emperor's status. Overjoyed, Yonai rushed to give the news on to the grand chamberlain.

It was just at this time that the draft for the new constitution was being prepared, and it took as its first premise the continuation of the imperial institution. But a dissatisfied GHQ claimed it represented no significant change from the existing Meiji Constitution, which provided for a weak representative body, a large centralized bureaucracy, and an emperor with many powers that lay outside governmental and even constitutional channels. They came up with some ideas of their own, which they passed on to the Japanese government to be used as the basis for a new draft. "The new constitution was written by MacArthur"—or so it could be said, but in any case Prime Minister Shidehara revised the document again, based on GHQ's suggestions, and won final approval from the Imperial Diet.

The most difficult struggle facing the writers was how to define the emperor's role in a way that would fall within the parameters of GHQ's wishes. After much vigorous debate, they finally settled on the word "symbol," used in several Western European constitutions. Article One read: "The emperor is a symbol of the state and of the unity of the people, deriving his position from the will of the people, with whom resides sovereign power." Thus, the emperor was no longer the sovereign, and his powers were greatly reduced. His right to appoint the prime minister and the chief justice of the Supreme Court, to promulgate laws and treaties, to dissolve the Diet, to preside over state ceremonies and receive foreign ambassadors and ministers, to confirm diplomatic documents, to confer honors, to grant amnesties and pardons—all became, under the new constitution, merely ceremonial activities.

The new constitution was approved by the Imperial Diet on November 3, 1946, and when it was put into effect on May 3 of the following year, some 100,000 people gathered in front of the palace to join the emperor and empress in commemorating the event. After the ceremonies were over, the citizens, delighted that a new era was opening up for them, surrounded the emperor's car, celebrating the new constitution and the fact that it legitimized the imperial institution.

***

While the imperial institution had been retained, the debate over Hirohito's responsibility for the war and his possible abdication continued to smolder. As soon as the war had ended, former prime minister Konoe immediately argued that Hirohito should abdicate. He felt that by doing so, and by returning to Kyoto and submitting himself to the judgment of the Allies, the emperor would make a favorable impression on GHQ and dispel any thoughts they might have of branding him a war criminal or abolishing the office. In his mind was the precedent of Yoshinobu Tokugawa, the last shogun, who in 1867 submitted to the Meiji Emperor, asking him to take back the reins of government.

It was from that time that Hirohito, who had always considered Konoe one of his closest advisers, began to lose confidence in him. It was not that the emperor disliked the idea of abdicating; rather, he feared that it would spark a great deal of unrest, too much for a still very young "Emperor Akihito" to handle.

There was also the view that precisely because Hirohito was emperor—whether a "symbol" or a participant—by virtue of his position he was not likely to be summoned into court as a witness, but if he were to abdicate and become an ordinary citizen, it could actually be worse for all concerned. This seems the more likely reason for his reluctance to leave office. But through his meetings with MacArthur,

Hirohito's anxieties about his own future were lessened. It seemed increasingly clear that he would stay on the throne. Yet, on January 4, 1946, just three days after he renounced his divinity, GHQ shocked the imperial household and the emperor himself by announcing a major purge of public officeholders.

It was an across-the-board purge, aimed at people in all walks of life who had actively promoted the war or had cooperated in its instigation. It also targeted ultranationalists. And GHQ did not stop with public officeholders. Not even the Special Police were immune. By the time it was over, some 210,000 had lost their jobs. The purge was so severe that Hirohito, barely able to control his agitation, said, "Surely this is a hint that I should abdicate." Fortunately he did not have to in the end.

The International Military Tribunal of the Far East began trials in May 1946. First to be charged were the twenty-eight Class "A" war criminals. Subsequently the presiding judge, Sir William Webb from Australia, and the judges and prosecutors from the other countries represented on the tribunal started to press for Hirohito's prosecution. At the very least they wanted him to appear before the court to testify in person.

At first Chief Prosecutor Joseph Keenan from the United States was the most vociferous of the group, but he had a sudden change of heart and ended up telling the others, "The prosecution will not bring charges against the emperor." Aghast, the prosecutors from the Soviet Union, the Philippines, Australia, and New Zealand protested vehemently, but Keenan could not be dissuaded.

The others countered. Taking their cross-examination of

169

former lord keeper of the privy seal Kido as an opportunity, they demanded that Hirohito be called as a witness, citing the numerous references to him in Kido's diary. But Keenan continued to resist.

His seemingly strange attitude stemmed from political concerns MacArthur held based on a secret investigation into the emperor's involvement. It was a result, too, of successful behind-the-scenes lobbying by Yasumasa Matsudaira of the Imperial Household Agency. (It was changed from a ministry to an agency within the prime minister's office in 1947.) Matsudaira, who had spent a lot of time in Europe and America, put his English-language skills and sociability to good use and succeeded in becoming close friends with Keenan. The parties he gave at his own home for Keenan, the duck-hunting outings he sponsored on imperial lands, and the art objects that he sent to the American might have had their effect in winning Keenan's sympathy. But Keenan's innate flexibility helped, too.

When Kido's lawyer was cross-examining Tōjō he asked, "Was there ever a time that Kido either acted in opposition to or spoke out against the emperor's wish [for peace]?"

Tōjō, throwing out his chest, replied, "There was never such a case. But beyond that, in Japan a subject, much less a high-ranking official, would never oppose the imperial will."

By insisting that a senior figure like Kido would never oppose the imperial will, Tōjō was in effect targeting Hirohito with responsibility for the war. The logical implication was that, if no one had opposed Hirohito, the war must have been undertaken in accordance with his wishes. Keenan turned pale. If the emperor were to be considered responsible for the war and were to be called to the stand as a witness, there was no telling what kind of unrest might result in Japan. Matsudaira, too, was aghast, and he and Keenan acted in secret to send a messenger to the jailed Tōjō explaining the problem to him. The ever-loyal Tōjō realized his mistake. During a subsequent cross-examination Keenan asked him a leading question: "Was it the emperor's desire to wage war?"

Tōjō replied as he was supposed to: "He may actually have been opposed to it, but in fact, he reluctantly followed my advice and went along with it. Nevertheless, until the very last moment, his was a peace-loving spirit. Even after the war had started he continued to feel that way."

Thus Tōjō shifted the responsibility for starting the war entirely onto himself, and shielded the emperor.

As far as the Far East tribunal was concerned, the principle was established that the emperor would not be charged or called to the witness stand. But the Soviets were still not satisfied with this. In February 1950 they suddenly raised a very difficult issue. It had to do with the old 731st Manchurian Unit, which had been experimenting with germ warfare under Lieutenant-General Ishii.

The Soviet ambassador in Washington, D.C., handed Secretary of State Acheson a diplomatic note: "Lieutenant-General Kajiwara, Chief of the Medical Corps for the Kwantung Army, has testified that in 1937 the 731st Unit in Manchuria was formed under special secret orders from Emperor Hirohito. We demand that the United States government order MacArthur to reconvene the International Tribunal and start proceedings against the four who masterminded this project, including the emperor and Ishii.''

The unit in question consisted of a number of doctors and scientists gathered under the cover of the Kwantung Army Water Sanitation Division and the Kwantung Army Veterinarian Division. In addition to research into biological and chemical weaponry, they also carried out inhumane and immoral experiments on thousands of Chinese and Allied prisoners-of-war, including such atrocities as injecting victims with germs and vivisecting them.

Obviously it was a matter that the Far East tribunal should have investigated, but due to strong objections from the U.S. Army, the matter was dropped. The U.S. side quickly gathered up all the secret data available on the subject for fear that it might fall into the hands of the Soviets.

Of course, the emperor could not have been the one to order the formation of such a group. In any case the Soviets had their own reasons for bringing the matter up. It was now five years after the end of the war, but the Russians were still forcibly detaining over 370,000 Japanese prisoners. By raising the Ishii issue they were hoping to embarrass MacArthur, who was clamoring for the return of those prisoners.

But this time, the Soviets found little support. Britain, and even Australia and the Philippines, who had been so steadfastly critical of Hirohito before, expressed their opposition to the Russian demands. The United States attacked pointedly: ''The one who amounts to a war criminal is Stalin, who refuses to repatriate the interned soldiers.''

However, the Communist party and the left wing in

Japan were persistently pursuing the question of Hirohito's war responsibility. Even the progressives outside the political arena followed this trend. Already, in April 1946, Shigeru Nanbara, president of Tokyo University, in a lecture entitled "On the Occasion of the Emperor's Birthday," boldly announced: "The emperor bears no political or legal responsibility [for the war] but I imagine that he must feel more than anyone else ethical and spiritual responsibility toward the imperial ancestors and the people of Japan."

In May of 1948, Supreme Court Chief Justice Shigeru Mibuchi said, "If at the end of the war the emperor had of his own accord issued a rescript accepting responsibility, it would have moved the Japanese people very deeply."

Along these same lines, Nanbara added a month later, in response to a query by a foreign reporter:

> I believe the emperor ought to abdicate. And I am not the only one; this is an opinion shared by educators throughout Japan, from elementary school teachers to university professors. The only thing is, he needs to consider the repercussions this would have among the Japanese people, and should time his announcement carefully. His abdication should be carried out without any pressure from politicians or citizens. It should be a spontaneous act that comes from within himself.

While the motivations of the military tribunal and the Communist party were vastly different, it is clear that a majority of Japanese felt somewhere in their hearts that Hirohito bore at least some measure of responsibility for the war, and the words of Nanbara and Mibuchi made a great impression.

173

But Prime Minister Shigeru Yoshida, ever the loyal retainer, could not stomach such suggestions. Indignant, he denounced Nanbara (who later opposed the peace treaty with the U.S. because it did not include the Soviets) as someone who would twist the truth in order to play up to public opinion. In so doing, he further stimulated public discussion of the question.

In any case, people believed that Hirohito, who was a scrupulous man, would abdicate of his own accord sooner or later. When the new constitution was proclaimed, when the trials for the Class "A" war criminals began (in February 1948), and again when the guilty were convicted and sentenced (in November and December of the same year), the media, both domestic and foreign, speculated anew about an abdication. But Hirohito just quietly rode out the storm.

The Crown Prince's Bride

"General MacArthur has been dismissed."

It was as if the sky had fallen. The Japanese, who are brought up to be submissive to authority, had eventually come to respect the supreme commander of their former enemies.

When Hirohito was first informed of the news at a little past 4 P.M. on April 11, 1951, he simply sat and stared into space for a long time. Later, when he had received more details from Grand Chamberlain Mitani, he seemed genuinely surprised again, saying, "So it's really true. . . ."

Six years before, in 1945, the emperor's fate had been in MacArthur's hands. And now the general had been relieved of his command with just one telegram from the president of the United States. With the outbreak of the Korean War in June 1950, MacArthur had been strongly urging the United States to stand up to China, which was backing North Korea, by moving into Manchuria, and also by involving the Nationalist Chinese army (on Taiwan) in the conflict. His continued insistence on this point put him at odds with President Truman, who finally lost patience with his intransigence. Truman feared that a widening conflict would bring in the Soviet Union and precipitate World War III.

"Old soldiers never die, they just fade away," said a dejected MacArthur when he returned to the United States. As he prepared to leave Japan, the emperor and the Imperial Household Agency had just one request. Until now, Hirohito had visited MacArthur ten times, but MacArthur had never once returned the courtesy by calling on the emperor. But this time the Imperial Household Agency let it be known that they would like the general to come to the palace to pay a farewell call. Now that MacArthur was just a retired soldier, it seemed like a reasonable request, but he flatly refused. Of course, one reason for his refusal must have been his innate sense of pride, but he also seems to have used the situation as a convenient outlet for his anger at Truman. Up until then his plan had been going along so well. He had hoped to win the Korean War, conclude a peace treaty with Japan, then, with those two great deeds behind him, return to the United States after more than ten years and offer himself as the Republican candidate for the presidency of the United States.

But one telegram brought it all to an inglorious end. It was not unreasonable for him to feel resentment about it, but he seemed to misdirect it. He would not even allow his wife to accept an invitation to the palace, and refused to accept an honor the emperor had hoped to bestow upon him. (On the latter score he did have a change of heart. After returning to the United States, he did accept the First Order of Merit with the Grand Cordon of the Rising Sun.)

Unavoidably, then, the emperor paid his eleventh call on MacArthur to thank him for his efforts on behalf of Japan. Once again Mrs. MacArthur was nowhere to be seen; in fact, she had never once come out to meet the emperor. However, the first time he came to visit, she and MacArthur's doctor had hidden behind the curtains and peeked at the proceedings.

On the day of the general's departure, June 16, 1951, a number of dignitaries, including Prime Minister Yoshida and Grand Chamberlain Mitani, were lined up at the airport to see him off. GHQ had strongly hinted that Hirohito should also be there, but as he had bade his farewells the day before at the embassy, he declined.

MacArthur quickly said his good-byes and boarded the plane. In the end he did not leave with any parting message for the Japanese people. But when, in his report to Congress after his return, he declared that "the spiritual age of the Japanese people is twelve years old," the admiration the Japanese had felt for him was dispelled in a moment, and all he left behind was a bitter aftertaste. Thus ended the "reign" of the man the Japanese called "the emperor outside the moat."

But if we look impartially at him as an administrator, his accomplishments were impressive: He solved the food shortages; he prevented a Communist revolution; he rebuilt the Japanese economy; and he maintained the imperial institution. If for nothing else Japan owes him an enormous debt of gratitude for averting the creation of "two Japans" by resisting Soviet pressure for a Russian occupation of Hokkaido.

With the end of the MacArthur era the Japanese felt a

great sense of liberation. His replacement, Lieutenant-General (later General) Matthew Ridgway, was a more easygoing type, as different as could be from MacArthur. After six stifling years of MacArthur's formality, people found Ridgway's more relaxed manner refreshing. He paid a courtesy call on the emperor; he and his wife visited Keio University together; and he was not reluctant to sign autographs. Perhaps the reason for this expansiveness was the economic recovery that had been triggered by the Korean conflict, and Ridgway's recognition of Japan's new role as a force for stability in Asia.

In September 1951, the long-awaited peace treaty was signed in San Francisco, and on April 28 of the following year, after seven years of occupation, Japan was an independent nation once more.

***

On November 10, 1952, ceremonies were held for Prince Akihito to mark his coming of age and formally install him as crown prince. While for most Japanese, "coming of age" occurs when they reach twenty, eighteen is the age of adulthood for emperors and crown princes. Akihito had actually turned eighteen on December 23 of the previous year, but the formal observance was delayed because the court was still in mourning for the Empress Dowager Teimei, Taishō's consort, who had died in the summer of 1951. Nineteen fifty-two was the year that the peace treaty was signed, and Japan was official host to numerous foreign dignitaries. Space was at a premium. The third floor of the Imperial Household Agency offices had been redone into apartments for Prince Akihito. The coming-of-age and installation ceremonies were held there, in the north reception room, which had only just been redecorated. They were the first national ceremonies to be held under the new constitution.

The emperor and the others in attendance wore traditional court dress and carried scepters, while the empress wore a short court robe over formal trousers such as were worn in the Heian period, and she too carried a scepter. Seated in the place of honor, the crown prince removed the cap that symbolized his minority. Then Hirohito placed an adult's headdress on his son's head. When this was done, Akihito approached his parents and formally announced his coming of age in a loud voice. The emperor and empress must have felt strong emotions at this moment. Bound by time-honored custom, they had entrusted his upbringing and education to others from an early age, and they had not seen that much of him as he grew up.

Just how infrequent their meetings were can be seen in an incident that occurred in 1945, when Akihito was still in the sixth grade of elementary school. It was November. Prince Akihito and his younger brother Prince Yoshi had been evacuated to Nikko, where they went to school until the end of the war. They returned to Tokyo and moved into a cottage near the imperial library, in the Fukiage Garden of the palace. They had been away for a year and a half, and had grown so much that their parents hardly recognized them.

That night Prince Akihito had gone to use the bath in the imperial library quarters, normally used by the emperor. As the young prince washed away the dirt from his travels, his father peeked in and said, smiling, "So, you're taking a

179

bath." It was the first time he had ever seen his son bathe. The two princes spent two nights in the cottage, regaling their parents with stories about their time in Nikko. It was a rare opportunity for the family to be together. One of their stories stunned and saddened the emperor. It seems that for a while after Hirohito's surrender broadcast, there was fear among the princes' aides that cadets from the Eastern Army, who frequented the Nikko barracks where the princes were housed and who remained determined to fight to the bitter end, might try to kidnap the princes.

In the spring of 1946, Prince Akihito finished elementary school. Times had changed since his father's youth, and no one felt he needed a special education at the palace. Instead he was sent to the Peers' Middle School in a suburb of Tokyo called Koganei. At that time the area around the school was still undeveloped, and the grassy Musashino Plain retained something of the poetic character for which it had been famous since ancient times.

There the young prince could lead a child's life, chasing butterflies through the mulberry fields and scooping fish from the streams. Yet, all was not sweet. Like other schoolboys, he was also hazed by the older bullies in the woods behind the school and forced to draw graffiti inside the lid of his desk. Because he was dark of complexion and a bit pudgy, his classmates nicknamed him "*Chabu,*" short for "*chabuta*" (brown pig). The name stuck for a long time. When his English teacher at the Peers' School, Mrs. Elizabeth Vining, gave him the nickname "Jimmy," he rejected it, saying with a proud smile, "I am the crown prince." He was not really offended, for he realized it was an American custom and that she'd meant no harm by it.

Akihito was a solitary child. He envied his friends their ordinary family lives and often seemed on the verge of tears. After school at the end of the day, there was no family house to return to, no doting parents ready to spoil him and ask him how his day had gone. Instead he was surrounded in his dormitory quarters by stiff old men who stood in awe of him and were always telling him what he should or should not do. There was no feeling of "home" among them. One of his school friends later said: "The atmosphere in his rooms was just like an office. It was the sort of place I could not stand."

When Akihito went on to high school, he declared to his friends, "When I get married, I will certainly have my children live at home with me." In other ways, too, the depth of his unhappiness was obvious. There was the time, for example, that he sneaked out of the dorm and went downtown to Ginza to wander around. And when his schoolmates stopped by to visit, they would often find him catching moths that flew in through the window, impaling them with a little knife, then pinning them in a line to the top of his desk. It seems that his father was simply incapable of understanding the young prince's feelings of isolation. There was a generation gap between Hirohito, who had accepted the restrictions of his position as something that custom demanded, and Akihito, the product of a new age. Now that the emperor had renounced his divinity, the Japanese would have been delighted to see the imperial family members all living under one roof, and indeed, Japan was the only country left in the world where the royal family lived apart. If Hirohito thought the imperial library too confining for the whole family, well, they could all have moved to the Akasaka Detached Palace. At some 108,000 square feet, with fifty-two rooms on the first two floors alone, there would have been plenty of space. But the emperor never took the initiative to bring his family together.

Shortly after being named crown prince, Akihito faced his first official duty, one which some thought might be too much for such a young man. He was to represent Japan at the coronation of Queen Elizabeth II. The Japanese, with stimulus from the Korean War, were recovering well from their defeat in World War II. They saw this occasion as a chance to regain international respect. Crown Prince Akihito left Yokohama on the American liner *President Wilson* on March 30, 1953. He was just nineteen and still a freshman in political science and economics at Gakushūin University. Interestingly enough, his father had also been nineteen when he first went to England thirty-two years before. On that previous trip Japan and England had been allies, and the reception for Hirohito had been accordingly warm. This time, however, Akihito was a visitor from a recent enemy, and there were those who still remembered the war vividly. In response to a *Daily Mail* newspaper opinion poll the day before his arrival, 68 percent said the crown prince should not have been invited to attend the coronation.

Comments in the poll ranged from "the crown prince ought to be held hostage until Japan makes full reparations to former British prisoners of war" to the dark humor of "I'd like to put *him* to work on the railroad," which was a reference to Japan's use of British war prisoners to build the Thailand-Burma railway during the war. Akihito was only allowed to visit Queen Elizabeth a week after the coronation ceremony, and even then it was treated as an unofficial call. On his sight-seeing visits he was greeted by hostile demonstrators from prisoner-of-war groups, and the Cambridge Hotel Association publicly refused lodgings to any Japanese. This must have pained the young prince, but he maintained his dignity and represented the Japanese people as best he could. At first the emperor had been excited about the trip. He'd bought a television so he could watch his son and, with pins on a map hung in his room, had charted Akihito's progress across the globe. But once the crown prince got to England, Hirohito became more subdued, and while he didn't say anything, it was obvious that the situation saddened him.

All in all, however, the prince did well in his fourteen-nation tour, meeting with kings and presidents and improving Japan's image abroad. When he returned to Japan six months later, the whole nation greeted him warmly. On October 15, some 50,000 people crammed into Hibiya Park near the palace to participate in a public celebration of his return.

***

His overseas trip had made Crown Prince Akihito very popular in Japan. He was nearing the age when a prince might customarily be expected to become engaged, and the media discovered there was money to be made in speculating publicly about a suitable bride for him. The newspapers all assigned reporters to the story, and everyone was looking for a scoop. They combed the country, looking for girls of good family, and extended their search to good universities as well. One paper even came up with a list of over 1,000 prospective candidates. This fierce competition continued for five years until a "cease-fire" of sorts was arranged so that Akihito could continue his education in peace. In any case, in the spring of 1958, the palace list was narrowed down to one: Michiko Shōda. This Japanese Cinderella story needs no retelling in Japan, but the "fateful day" was August 19, 1957. The Prince had gone to Karuizawa to play tennis, and on that day he "by chance" found himself across the net from Michiko in a doubles match. Most people now agree that one of the crown prince's teachers, the economist Shinzō Koizumi, who knew the Shōda family, set the whole thing up.

In any case, it was love at first sight for the crown prince. She was everything Akihito had told his school friends he was looking for: beautiful, intelligent, charming, and outgoing. After returning from Karuizawa, the two played tennis again several times in Tokyo. The following summer they were back in Karuizawa again, with a group of school friends, and it was obvious they were falling in love. That August 20 the crown prince's office sent a messenger to the Shōda family to make a formal proposal. The stunned family held a conference, and everyone was opposed to the match. Michiko's elder brother was especially adamant. Their main worry was that because they were commoners, the marriage could cause difficulties within the imperial family, which was the guardian of tradition and custom. They also feared that Michiko would become the object of jealousy and ill-feeling among aristocratic families and distant members of the imperial house, whose own daughters

184

might have married the crown prince. In short, they would have much preferred their daughter to make an ordinary, happy marriage.

On September 3 the Shōda family abruptly announced that Michiko was off to Brussels, ostensibly for an international meeting of students from Sacred Heart Schools. They said that she was being sent as Japan's representative to the conference, but the real reason was to protect her from publicity and to hint at their refusal of the proposal. On the day of her departure, the crown prince, not willing to give up so easily, apparently sent her, through a mutual friend, a stream of letters in which he pleaded his case. He also telephoned the Shōda residence any number of times. For her part, Michiko returned from her travels determined to marry Akihito no matter what the difficulties.

In the middle of November the Shōda family acquiesced and formally announced their acceptance of the proposal, and shortly thereafter the proposed match was put before a conference of imperial family members, at which several political leaders were also present. Michiko's family and educational background, the circumstances of her home life, and her distant relatives were discussed in minute detail. Michiko had graduated in English Literature from Seishin (Sacred Heart) Women's University. Her academic performance had been outstanding; she had served as student body president; and she was popular among her classmates. Her family was well known and successful. There were almost no objections among the conferees, although Diet President Nobusuke Kishi raised one issue: "The imperial family follows Shinto, but the Shōda family is Christian. Does anyone see a problem there?"

Takeshi Usami, the head of the Imperial Household Agency, replied, "It is true that her family is Christian, and the school that she attended is Catholic, but Michiko herself has not been baptized. I imagine that she can convert to Shinto."

This satisfied the conferees, and the marriage was accepted. Shortly after the meeting adjourned, the Imperial Household Agency announced the engagement, settling once and for all the superheated media speculation about the crown prince's marriage prospects.

Symbol of the New Japan

From the late 1950s, the pace of Japan's economic development accelerated dramatically, bringing with it a marked improvement in the Japanese standard of living. The Imperial Household Agency felt the time was right to begin rebuilding the imperial palace, much of which was still in ruins from the war. During the war, makeshift repairs had been carried out on Hirohito's quarters in the former imperial library, but perhaps because of the insulation that had been laid between the two ceilings, the rooms got unbearably humid. At times condensation would drip from the walls and electrical wiring. Palace aides fretted about the health of their imperial charges, but the emperor kept insisting that the time was not right for rebuilding, which should wait until the nation was in better shape. So the work was put off, although in 1953 some major improvements were carried out, which included adding rooms for palace staff. However, the Imperial Household Agency still tried to maintain the emperor's image as "living in a makeshift air raid shelter."

Taking advantage of the imperial family's increased public popularity, the Imperial Household Agency decided to rebuild the palace completely. Work began in 1959. The new structure, called the Fukiage Palace, which was completed in November 1961, lay just south of the old imperial library. It was an elegant cream-colored structure covering roughly 14,400 square feet, with one underground level and two floors aboveground connected by an elevator, out of consideration for the imperial couple's advancing age. The family moved in on December 8.

The emperor, ever the scholar, was especially pleased with the large new library, which was large enough to hold his many academic books and monographs, as well as books on the imperial family. He was also delighted because, unlike his former quarters on the ground floor, his second-floor bedroom overlooked the Fukiage Garden.

In addition to these residential apartments, a new Palace Hall was needed. Starting with the visits of Vice-President Nixon in 1953 and Ethiopian Emperor Haile Selassie in 1956, it became clear that Japan could expect an increasing number of state visitors and diplomats. Japan needed an appropriate place in which to formally receive these visitors, a place that both reflected the nation's growing prosperity and gave suitable diplomatic weight to the imperial household. For lack of anything better, they had been using the redecorated third floor of the Imperial Household Agency offices for receptions, but this space was cramped and not nearly grand enough for these purposes. For the sake of Japan's honor, it was decided that the Palace Hall should be rebuilt. Planning began in 1960, ground was broken in 1964, and the hall was completed in the fall of 1968.

The grand and gaudy edifices of the recent past were rejected in favor of a simpler Japanese-style design of quieter dignity. The total floor space was 250,000 square feet, and building costs came to 13.3 billion yen. Reflecting the automobile age, a 124-space parking garage was constructed under the east garden. Workers even cleared and replanted a vegetable garden that had stood on the site of the burnt-out ruins of the old Meiji Palace and had been used to supply the household with food during the days of scarcity following the war. As a result of all the reconstruction, sections of the old Edo castle site on which the palace stood were opened to the public.

Since the war, the left wing had long complained that at 260 acres (excluding the outer parks and moats), the palace grounds were just too large and that part of them should be made available for public use. As a compromise and in return for the public expense of rebuilding the palace living quarters and reception hall, outer sections of the old grounds were opened as public parks.

***

Hirohito began touring the country in February 1946. By 1951, after a series of trips, he had visited the islands of Honshu, Shikoku, and Kyushu. Hokkaido was left off the itinerary for security reasons, but finally, in 1954, the emperor went there for a national athletic meet. On his return, he flew on an airplane for the first time. His delighted response was straightforward: "I never knew it could be this comfortable." In any case, with his trip to Hokkaido, his pledge to tour the entire country (not counting the various smaller islands) was virtually fulfilled. There was only Okinawa left, but the island was still under United States military occupation.

In 1953, Amami Oshima was returned to Japanese control, and in 1968 the Ogasawara Islands also reverted. The movement to have Okinawa revert was growing year by year, but the U.S. saw their bases on the island as the keystone in their Pacific strategy of keeping the Soviet Union and China in check. For national security reasons they were afraid to let the island out of their control. But finally, after twenty-seven years of negotiations by a string of prime ministers, Okinawa was returned to Japan in 1972.

Historically it is very rare indeed for one country to return occupied territory to another on the basis of harmonious diplomatic negotiations. Japan need only look north to the Kuril Islands, still under Soviet control, to understand this. If those islands had been under American jurisdiction after the war, by now they would be back in Japan's hands. Nevertheless, however happy "mainland" Japanese may have been about the reversion, the feelings of the Okinawans themselves were rather more complicated. From the fourteenth century onward Okinawa had been an independent kingdom, but they were subsequently invaded and subjugated by the Satsuma warlords of southern Kyushu, who ruled the islands until the Meiji Restoration in 1868.

Then, in World War II, it became Japan's last line of defense, and even Okinawan schoolchildren took up arms in the name of the emperor and provided medical support for the Japanese soldiers in the field. In light of the tragedy it was thought that the emperor ought to visit Okinawa when the islands were returned to Japan. Yet, for some reason, Hirohito continued to hesitate. In the summer of 1965, at the Nasu Detached Palace, the emperor was at a regularly scheduled press conference with the palace press corps. At one point he was asked, "Your Majesty has traveled throughout the country but still has not visited Okinawa. The Okinawan people themselves have said they'd like you to come. . . ."

Hirohito parried, "You say I have traveled all over the country, but in fact I have not. I still haven't visited some of the Izu islands, Tsushima, the Goto Islands, and the Satsunan Islands. I should like to see all of them too." By way of putting an end to this line of questioning, he went on to say, "I have not heard anything about the Okinawan people wanting me to come. In any case, there are still problems with Okinawa's status, so I am unable to say at this time whether or not I will go."

His security people had been against a trip because revolutionary fervor was running high in Okinawa, and they feared a strong anti-imperial sentiment. On the other hand it seemed that it might actually be good policy for Hirohito to risk the trip, to thank the Okinawan people for their efforts on his behalf, and to pay his respects at the Himeyuri Pagoda war memorial. Still, it was Crown Prince Akihito who ended up making this initial visit, three years after Okinawa had been returned to Japanese control. In 1975 he went to Okinawa to attend the opening ceremonies for the Okinawa Oceanic Exposition as honorary president of the organizing committee. Normally this would have been a role for the emperor to play, but Akihito performed admirably. He had long had an interest in Okinawa. Whenever scholars came to the palace to lecture on Okinawa, he had listened with great interest, and he made it a point to invite visiting Okinawan children to the palace every year so that he could talk to them. When it was decided that he should make a trip there, he said, "Even if they throw stones at me, I'd like to at least try and get to know the people there."

As soon as he and Princess Michiko landed in Okinawa's largest city of Naha, they went first to the Himeyuri Pagoda. As husband and wife presented a bouquet of flowers at the monument and paused to observe a moment of silence, they were suddenly startled by the sound of Molotov cocktails and stones being thrown. Flames shot up around them. The attackers were two student extremists who had been hiding in a trench behind the memorial since the previous day. Akihito reacted to the incident with aplomb. He calmly paid his respects at two other memorial pagodas, and after making a condolence call on a group of relatives of the war dead, he gave a short speech that greatly moved the local people and revealed the deepest feelings of the "mainland" Japanese toward Okinawa:

> Though in the past visited with great suffering, Okinawa has remained firm in its desire for peace. During the last war its people found themselves in the midst of the only battlefield on Japanese soil, and their great and tragic sacrifices must never be forgotten. When I think of the victims and their bereaved families, I am overwhelmed with feelings of sadness. I believe that we must always keep in mind the painful history of Okinawa and bear witness to the scars of its

people. We must work together to rebuild. The noble sacrifices Okinawa has made cannot be redeemed by the deeds and words of a single day. We must retain these sacrifices forever in our memories, and reflect upon them deeply, and only then can we truly understand Okinawa.

When the crown prince and his consort departed from Okinawa two days later, several thousand people came to give them a warm send-off at Naha Airport. But Emperor Hirohito himself never did visit Okinawa.

***

Once, when asked what his fondest memory was, Hirohito replied without hesitation that it was the trip he took to Europe in his youth. He had been particularly impressed with England, and in 1969, when he saw an exhibition called "Tradition and Progress in England," he was reminded again of his visit nearly half a century before. Thus, when it was announced that the emperor and empress, having served the nation so selflessly for so long, would go to Europe while their health still permitted them to enjoy it, both the Imperial Household Agency and the Japanese people were delighted. By now Japan was universally acknowledged as a world power economically, so much so that one American scholar had stated that the twenty-first century belonged to Japan. So wealthy had Japan become that office secretaries and even the wives and children of farming families now strolled the streets of Paris. By the spring of 1971, plans were in place. The imperial couple were to be gone for eighteen days, from September 27 to

October 14. Their visits to England, Belgium, and West Germany would be official state occasions, but excursions to Denmark, France, the Netherlands, and Switzerland would be informal.

The day of the departure was clear, and at a refueling stop in Alaska along the way, then U.S. president Nixon and his wife flew all the way to Anchorage to greet the imperial couple. The emperor and empress also received a smiling welcome from Denmark's King Frederik IX when they arrived in Copenhagen. Such warm receptions must have rekindled nostalgia in the emperor for his earlier European tour.

But among some Europeans there was still a deep-rooted coolness, or even outright hostility, toward this Japanese visitor. The intensity of anti-Japanese sentiment in England and the Netherlands was to some degree expected. But even in Denmark, which was the first stop on their tour, demonstrators threw feces at the emperor and passed out anti-Hirohito handbills. In England one man threw his overcoat at the open car in which Hirohito was riding along with Queen Elizabeth. In another incident a commemorative Japanese cedar the emperor had planted during the visit was chopped down one night, and hydrochloric acid was poured on its roots. The worst was in the Netherlands. There the windshield of Hirohito's car was cracked when someone threw a bottle at it. The Japanese flag was burned, and windows were broken at the embassy residence. The Dutch had lost Indonesia during the war, and their POWs had been cruelly treated by the Japanese. Their resentment ran very deep. The emperor was greeted by shouts and placards proclaiming "Hirohito go home!" "Fascist murderer," "Give me back my dead father," and "For the sake of the friend I lost in a POW camp, I now protest this visit by his killer." In Belgium and even in Germany, which had been Japan's ally, people threw tomatoes at the emperor and empress, and there were numerous demonstrations.

At a public banquet in his honor in Great Britain, Queen Elizabeth proclaimed, "Our two nations have not always had peaceful relations in the past. However, the bonds which were first cultivated between us during my late grandfather's day have strengthened, and I believe we will not make the same mistake twice."

Yet, in his reply, Hirohito expressed no regrets for Japan's involvement in the war, and this stirred indignation among the British. It is often said that the English forgive but never forget, and on the day the emperor left for the Netherlands, all their pent-up anger towards him came out in the newspapers:

> The emperor who stood and spoke at Her Majesty's banquet last night is the same one who ruled when British soldiers were taken prisoner and used to build the Burma Railroad. The past cannot be swept aside in the name of protocol surrounding an official visit. [*The Guardian*]

> The emperor's words were filled with an empty geniality, as if relations between our two nations have always been fine. Why did we hear no expression of regret? [*The Daily Telegraph*]

"The emperor's words" had in fact been carefully crafted by the Imperial Household Agency and the ministry of foreign affairs, then revised by Hirohito himself. It is perhaps unfortunate that he did not have better advice in this case.

Yet not everyone was hostile. There were some who looked with surprise at the emperor, who was so clearly sincere, and thought to themselves, "This is the 'son of heaven' as he was called by those fanatics in the Japanese army?! I thought he would look more like Hitler. . . ." And all in all, his presence seemed to confirm the adage "One visit by the king is worth 100 ambassadors."

Four years later, in 1975, Queen Elizabeth and Prince Philip paid a return visit to Japan. The British royal family had been a model for the Japanese imperial house since the Meiji era. The queen arrived on a lovely day in May, and during her six-day stay captured the hearts of the Japanese people. On the third day, at the queen's suggestion, she rode in an open car for the 1.9 kilometers between the Imperial Hotel and the National Theater. Undaunted by an unfortunate transportation strike, several tens of thousands of people lined the route to see her. Her unaffected smile and unassailable dignity and grace remained with the Japanese long after she had returned to England.

In the autumn of 1975 the emperor and empress set off on a trip to the United States. Ostensibly it was a courtesy visit, returning U.S. President Ford's visit to Japan in November of the previous year, but both the emperor and the Japanese people viewed it as an opportunity formally to express gratitude to the United States. The fact is, Japan's ability to rebuild itself after World War II owed a great deal to the United States, and now, thirty years later, Hirohito saw that the time was right for him to go to America and express his thanks.

But the journey had not easily come to fruition. In 1960, Eisenhower had planned to come to Japan, but just a few days before his arrival the government was forced to call the trip off. Left-wing riots against the U.S.–Japan Security Treaty, up for renewal in 1960, had created a state of unrest in Japan so serious that some thought a revolution was imminent. When Eisenhower's press secretary Haggerty came to Japan to make advance arrangements, his car was surrounded by demonstrators ten and twenty deep at Haneda Airport. He was trapped for an hour and ten minutes and finally had to be rescued by helicopter. The situation was too explosive to permit a presidential visit.

Thirteen years later, in the spring of 1973, Prime Minister Kakuei Tanaka prematurely announced that the emperor would be going to the United States that coming October. Imperial Household Agency Chief Usami was beside himself with anger. The Imperial Household Agency was merely a section of the Prime Minister's Office, but Usami—sometimes called "Emperor Usami" behind his back—had been its head for more than twenty years, and he was not about to let the prime minister steal the show.

Besides, October was the month that the Grand Shrine at Ise was to be rededicated. It is rebuilt every twenty years, and its rededication is one of the emperor's most sacred functions. So the October trip was out of the question.

Then, in February of 1974, Ambassador to the United States Takeshi Yasukawa announced to a group of reporters that Hirohito was going to come to the United States sometime that year, adding when he could see they doubted him, "This isn't just a rumor. You can lay money on it."

This put the government and the ruling party in a very awkward position. There was a story behind Ambassador Yasukawa's announcement. In August of 1973, Prime Minister Tanaka had already given informal consent to an imperial visit when President Nixon brought it up at their meeting in Hawaii. Subsequently the Lockheed scandal in Japan and Watergate in the United States had compromised the two leaders. Now, more than ever, an imperial visit was important to them. Nixon hoped it would shore up his waning popularity, while Tanaka wanted the trip to happen as soon as possible to save his own face, especially after having announced it prematurely the year before.

At this point the public began to react with disgust to the obvious use of the emperor for political purposes, and the ambassador was forced to back down on his earlier statement, saying, "I was under a mistaken impression." The incident even caused the vice-minister of foreign affairs to resign.

After all this political nonsense, the emperor's trip finally came to pass, and it turned out much better than even the most optimistic predictions. Top politicians from the president on down gave Hirohito the warmest of welcomes, and the American people, too, true to their nature, received him with open arms. Part of the reason for this enthusiastic reception lay in America's view of Japan as the "honor student" among the allies. But beyond that, there was a great deal of curiosity among ordinary citizens about this mysterious "emperor" whose line had reigned for 2,000 years. And finally, they responded to an image of the

Japanese nation (no longer just one of kamikaze pilots) rising like a phoenix from the utter defeat of World War II.

This time the Japanese were determined not to repeat the mistake they had made in England. At the White House banquet in the emperor's honor, President Ford made no mention of the war in his remarks, but Hirohito did: "And there is something else I would like to express to the people of this nation. Immediately after that unfortunate war, for which I am profoundly saddened, your nation lent ours a warm and helping hand in the rebuilding of Japan. . . ." The statement was met with prolonged applause.

Behind the Chrysanthemum Curtain

On October 31, 1975, a little more than two weeks after his return from the United States, Emperor Hirohito gave a press conference in the imperial palace. Since he had met with reporters several times in the United States, the Japanese press was clamoring for equal treatment. Although he met with the regular palace press corps once a year, this was the first time he had an open press conference, and with television cameras broadcasting it live throughout Japan, it was an epoch-making event. Still, it would be hard to call it a complete success.

One newsman, referring to the fact the Hirohito had mixed freely with the American public while he was there, tried to draw the emperor out with "There is among Japanese, too, a wish that Your Majesty might mingle more informally, and more often, with the people here."

But Hirohito's reply, which seemed strange considering his tour of Japan during the Occupation, was: "I would like to do such a thing if I could, but there is a great difference between the Japanese national character and the American national character. I seriously doubt I would be able to travel throughout the Japan like a tourist, as I did in the United States.''

Another reporter asked, ''There are many in Japan who lost parents, children, and spouses during the war yet, rose from the ashes and worked to rebuild Japan. What words do you have for them?''

The emperor responded, ''To them I say this: Every year on August 15 I recall that time with great pain. And I now rejoice that these same people, who suffered so much, have contributed to Japan's development.''

This triggered a string of unrehearsed questions. (Up to that point the questions asked had been submitted in advance.) A Japanese reporter with the London *Times* asked, ''When Your Majesty was at the White House, you referred to 'that unfortunate war, for which I am profoundly saddened.' Are we to interpret that as an expression of your responsibility for the war? Just what are your thoughts on the question of wartime responsibility?''

Hirohito was taken aback and took a moment to answer in a way that did not address the question very directly. ''As for the subtle nuances of my remark, not being a specialist in things literary, I am afraid they are beyond me. I am not really able to respond to your question.''

When a journalist asked him about the dropping of the atomic bomb, he said, ''I feel that it was truly regrettable that the atomic bomb was dropped. But it was in the midst of a war, and however tragic it may have been for the citizens of Hiroshima, I believe it was unavoidable.''

This caused great consternation for Usami, who tried mightily after the press conference to explain it away as a slip of the tongue. At the annual meetings with the palace press corps, he was accustomed to being able to jump up and close off the proceedings if a difficult question was asked, but this time it was a live event, and he could do nothing at the time. (As feared, the word "unavoidable" drew sharp reaction from victims of the bombing and the citizens of Hiroshima, and strong protests from the Communist party.)

In any case, the television screen showed to the Japanese the image of an emperor, once revered as a "living god," now unveiled. It was the image of a serious, shy man sitting erect, his hands on his knees, his small head nodding back and forth as he stuttered and searched for words. As an editorial in the magazine *Shūkan Shinchō* put it: "The press conference was not what we had expected. . . . The newspapers carried full accounts, with detailed explanations of the event, but the image shown on television had its own power and impact."

Every summer the palace press corps was allowed a roughly thirty-minute "press conference" with the emperor in the grounds of the Nasu Detached Palace. Of course, the Imperial Household Agency refused to call it a press conference. Their view was that "sometimes the emperor, as he was strolling through the garden, would stop and chat awhile with the reporters." But the fact is, the day was fixed in advance, and the reporters submitted their questions in writing some days beforehand. Then a press attaché rehearsed the emperor's answers with him. The head of the Imperial Household Agency and other important agency officials came down from Tokyo especially for the occasion. The interview itself was recorded on tape, and afterward officials went over the tape with the reporters, "revising" sections that the emperor might have misspoken and negotiating with the press as to what would be reported.

The interview in 1977 was a rare instance when the circumstances surrounding the end of the war became the focus of the questioning. One reporter asked, "Is it true that referring to Emperor Meiji's Charter Oath in the preface to your renunciation of divinity was your own idea?"

Hirohito responded at length:

> In fact, the main aim of the declaration was to reiterate the Charter Oath. The question of my divinity was secondary. . . . It was Emperor Meiji who first introduced democracy to Japan, and I felt there was a great need to assert that democracy was not just some imported concept. So that Japan would not forget what it had to be proud of, the purpose of the declaration was to remind the people of Emperor Meiji's fine ideas.

Another reporter asked, "The Potsdam Declaration included the provision that Japan's government should be freely elected by the people. As this called into question the traditional national polity, why did you so readily accept the conditions laid down?"

Again, Hirohito's reply was long:

> With regards to the so-called national polity—in other words, the imperial house—that house has ruled in an unbroken line for centuries only by virtue of the trust and faith of the people. This can be seen, for example, in the way that such military leaders as Mōri

Motonari and Oda Nobunaga honored and came to the aid of the imperial house, which had fallen on hard times during the Warring States period. For its part, the imperial house has always thought of the Japanese people as its children. That has been our traditional view, and it is for that reason that I accepted the conditions so readily.

These revelations were spread across the front pages of all the newspapers, and engendered mixed and complicated feelings among the Japanese people. What were they to make of the idea that the emperor's renunciation of his divinity, which was so shocking at the time, was "secondary" to his main purpose in making the announcement?

Nothing could have demonstrated more clearly that a "chrysanthemum curtain" had been drawn around the emperor ever since the war. The papers were nearly unanimous in attacking Hirohito's lack of understanding of the world around him.

The emperor's "guard dog," Usami, made his irritation at all this clear when he vowed, "As long as I live, I will never permit [a press conference] again." And in fact there was no press conference the following summer, but intermediaries intervened, and another one was held at the end of the year.

***

In November 1976, a ceremony commemorating Hirohito's fifty years on the throne was held at Tokyo's Budokan Hall. But it did not take place without controversy. To be sure, most Japanese did not think twice about expressing straightforward felicitations on his longevity and rule. Yet, many were against celebrating the event. Yes, they argued, the thirty years since the war had been good, but they could not overlook the fact that it was the same emperor who had reigned over the twenty dark years before that.

The Socialist and Communist parties as usual led the opposition, and they found an ally in Tokyo's governor Ryōkichi Minobe, a champion of reformist causes. He announced that he would not attend the ceremony. Reformist mayors throughout the country followed his lead, with leftists and intellectuals voicing their support for the move. National opinion was split down the middle.

The government, which was organizing the event, scaled it down in response to the public outcry. A third group emerged suggesting that the emperor could turn public opinion around if he were to thank those who wished to fete him, then decline the honor of the ceremony. They added that if Hirohito had issued a formal apology to the Japanese people right after the war, there would not be such an uproar today, and the issue of his wartime responsibility would have long since faded into the background.

Amid this controversy the ceremony was held as scheduled. Seven thousand five hundred attended, including politicians, bureaucrats, and foreign dignitaries. Security was tight—helicopters hovering overhead, and five hundred policemen, with supporting armored vehicles, outside. Hirohito was not unmindful of the feelings the event had generated, and in his remarks at the ceremony he added the following: "When I think of the many people, and their families, who sacrificed their lives during the war, and when I further see that the wounds of that war remain with us today, the grief it causes me is almost more than I can bear.''

At the time, people assumed that this fiftieth anniversary ceremony would be the last such for Hirohito, but happily his health held up, and ten years later a sixtieth anniversary celebration was held. This time there was little opposition; most people gladly offered their congratulations to the emperor and wished him continued good health.

***

When historians look back a hundred years from now, surely they will count Hirohito as one of the handful of Japanese emperors—like Tenchi, Go-Daigo, and Meiji—who stood out among the 124 who have reigned over the centuries. He was perhaps not one of the wisest and most decisive of Japan's rulers, but his honest virtue as a champion of peace and international harmony stood out for over sixty years, including his time as regent. Yet, his tragic flaw was his inability to exercise his power as commander in chief and check the rampaging excesses of his military esrablishment, which sought to subjugate the Asian continent, not realizing that the age of colonialism was past.

Emperor Meiji was strong-minded by nature, and in addition was surrounded by a stellar group of leaders. In contrast, Emperor Hirohito's temperament was fastidious and scholarly, and those around him were not especially decisive. It was his great misfortune that he seemed doomed to a life of isolation and pain. If we can divide rulers into pacifist types and those who relish pressure, Hirohito is undoubtedly one of the former.

In the end it was fortunate for both Hirohito and the Japanese people that after the war the emperor was stripped of most of his powers and became a national symbol, as evidenced by the course Japan has taken in the forty-some years since the war. A new, transformed, "human" emperor went out among the people right after the war, touring the country, meeting and talking to its citizens face-to-face. This led many to expect that the Japanese imperial family would eventually become more open, as European monarchies had. But in a few short years, after the Occupation forces left, a "chrysanthemum curtain" was pulled down around the Japanese ruler, and his contacts with the people grew infrequent.

Moreover, hiding behind his prestige, his aides in the Imperial Household Agency began to throw their weight around, treating even local politicians arrogantly when the emperor was on tour. As years passed, the security around him grew tighter. The excuse was that the world was becoming an ever more dangerous place, but surely nothing could have been more dangerous for Hirohito than those two or three years just after the war when he was traveling around the country with a minimal retinue.

Increased security was not the only thing. There seemed to be a nonchalant effort being made to reinstitute the divine aura around him. For example, in the past, whenever the emperor spoke at some occasion or the other, he would casually pull the written speech from his pocket and begin reading from it, but as time went on, a chamberlain began carrying his speeches for him. When it

207

came time to speak, the chamberlain would make an elaborate show of taking the speech out and presenting it to Hirohito, and after the emperor was finished, the chamberlain would take the speech back with equal pomposity. As the emperor became more and more distant from the people, they in turn felt increasingly disappointed.

It is safe to say that there is a wide range of opinion among Japanese regarding Hirohito's responsibility for the war. No matter how much he seemed to desire peace, he did approve the war plans that were discussed at the imperial conferences in late 1941; his signature appears on the declaration of war; and he gave his consent to the attack on Pearl Harbor. As a consequence, over 3,000,000 Japanese soldiers died, and several millions were wounded in battle; some 9,550,000 civilians were killed or wounded in the air raids over Japan; and millions more had to be repatriated from Japan's former colonies. Even now, more than forty years later, there are many who still suffer both psychologically and physically.

That Hirohito escaped trial at the Far Eastern War Crimes Tribunal was solely because it was politically expedient for America and the Occupation forces. But this by no means absolves him. As noted earlier, there is a feeling among many that if he had apologized and taken public responsibility just after the war, the matter would now be behind Japan. And it is unfortunate that between 1952 and 1975, Hirohito visited the Yasukuni Shrine only seven times to honor the war dead. To be sure, part of the reason for the infrequency of his visits was that they put the ruling party in an embarrassing political position, but it is sad nonetheless.

I suspect that when all is said and done, historians will have this to say about Emperor Hirohito: He may have been of pure and noble character, but for some reason he never found it in himself to accept responsibility for the war.

Prime Ministers and Cabinets, 1912–1989

Prime Minister	Cabinet Number	Cabinet Term
Tarō Katsura	3rd	21 December 1912–20 February 1913
Gonnohyōe Yamamoto	1st	20 February 1913–16 April 1914
Shigenobu Ōkuma	2nd	16 April 1914–9 October 1916
Masatake Terauchi		9 October 1916–29 September 1918
Takashi Hara		29 September 1918–13 November 1921
Korekiyo Takahashi		13 November 1921–12 June 1922
Tomasaburō Katō		12 June 1922–2 September 1923
Gonnohyōe Yamamoto	2nd	2 September 1923–7 January 1924
Keigo Kiyoura		7 January–1924–11 June 1924
Takaaki Katō	1st	11 June 1924–2 August 1925
Takaaki Katō	2nd	2 August 1925–30 January 1926
Reijirō Wakatsuki	1st	30 January 1926–20 April 1927
Giichi Tanaka		20 April 1927–2 July 1929
Osachi Hamaguchi		2 July 1929–14 April 1931
Reijirō Wakatsuki	2nd	14 April 1931–13 December 1931
Tsuyoshi Inukai		13 December 1931–16 May 1932
Makoto Saitō		16 May 1932–8 July 1934
Keisuke Okada		8 July 1934–9 March 1936
Kōki Hirota		9 March 1936–2 February 1937
Senjūrō Hayashi		2 February 1937–4 June 1937
Fumimaro Konoe	1st	4 June 1937–5 January 1939
Kiichirō Hiranuma		5 January 1939–30 August 1939
Nobuyuki Abe		30 August 1939–16 January 1940
Mitsumasa Yonai		16 January 1940–22 July 1940
Fumimaro Konoe	2nd	22 july 1940–18 July 1941
Fumimaro Konoe	3rd	18 July 1941–18 October 1941
Hideki Tōjō		18 October 1941–22 July 1944
Kuniaki Koiso		22 July 1944–7 April 1945
Kantarō Suzuki		7 April 1945–17 August 1945
Naruhiko Higashikuni		17 August 1945–9 October 1945

Prime Minister	Cabinet Number	Cabinet Term
Kijūrō Shidehara		9 October 1945–22 May 1946
Shigeru Yoshida	1st	22 May 1946–24 May 1947
Tetsu Katayama		24 May 1947–10 March 1948
Hitoshi Ashida		10 March 1948–15 October 1948
Shigeru Yoshida	2nd	15 October 1948–16 February 1949
Shigeru Yoshida	3rd	16 February 1949–30 October 1952
Shigeru Yoshida	4th	30 October 1952–21 May 1953
Shigeru Yoshida	5th	21 May 1953–10 December 1954
Ichirō Hatoyama	1st	10 December 1954–19 March 1955
Ichirō Hatoyama	2nd	19 March 1955–22 November 1955
Ichirō Hatoyama	3rd	22 November 1955–23 December 1956
Tanzan Ishibashi		23 December 1956–25 February 1957
Nobusuke Kishi	1st	25 February 1957–12 June 1958
Nobusuke Kishi	2nd	12 june 1958–19 july 1960
Hayato Ikeda	1st	19 July 1960–8 December 1960
Hayato Ikeda	2nd	8 December 1960–9 December 1963
Hayato Ikeda	3rd	9 December 1963–9 November 1964
Eisaku Satō	1st	9 November 1964–17 February 1967
Eisaku Satō	2nd	17 February 1967–14 January 1970
Eisaku Satō	3rd	14 January 1970–7 July 1972
Kakuei Tanaka	1st	7 July 1972–22 December 1972
Kakuei Tanaka	2nd	22 December 1972–9 December 1974
Takeo Miki		9 December 1974–24 December 1976
Takeo Fukuda		24 December 1976–7 December 1978
Masayoshi Ōhira	1st	7 December 1978–9 November 1979
Masayoshi Ōhira	2nd	9 November 1979–17 July 1980
Zenkō Suzuki		17 July 1980–27 November 1982
Yasuhiro Nakasone	1st	27 November 1982–27 December 1983
Yasuhiro Nakasone	2nd	27 December 1983–22 July 1986
Yasuhiro Nakasone	3rd	22 July 1986–6 November 1987
Noboru Takeshita		6 November 1987–3 June 1989

INDEX

Abe, Nobuyuki, 99–100
Akasaka Detached Palace, 41–42, 182
Akihito, Crown Prince: birth of, 92–93; childhood of, 93–95, 179–81; coming of age of, 178–79; education of, 180; engagement and marriage of, 183–86; eulogy to Emperor Shōwa (Hirohito) of, 4; visit to Britain of, 182–83; visit to Okinawa of, 191–93
Anami, Korechika, 128, 130, 132, 133, 136
Andō, Teruzō, 69, 74
Anglo-Japanese Alliance, 12, 30
Araki, Sadao, 73

Britain: 25, 29–30, 97; visit of Crown Prince Akihito to, 182–83; visit of Emperor Hirohito to, 29–32, 193, 194, 195
Bryce, Reginald, 157

Changkufeng, 84–87
Chang Tso-Lin, 49, 50–51, 53, 79
Charter Oath of Five Articles, 158, 203
Chichibu, Prince, 15, 16, 62, 74–76, 92
China, 11, 12, 25, 49–50, 57, 81–89, 103–4

"chrysanthemum curtain," 204, 207
Communist party, 150–51, 163, 172, 202, 205
Constitution, postwar, 166–68
coronation, of Emperor Hirohito, 45–46, 54–55

earthquake, of 1923, 40
Edward, Prince of Wales, 30–31, 37–38
emperors: accession of, 28–29, 44–45; constitutional powers of, 52–53, 65–67, 79, 86–87, 100, 167–68; medical treatment of, 2–3, 19; mythological divinity of, 2–3, 61, 156–57, 158
"Emperor's Proclamation of His Humanity, The," 158–59, 203
Europe, visit of Emperor Hirohito to, 28–33, 193–96

February 26 Incident, 68–80
Fellers, Bonner, 144–45
France, visit of Emperor Hirohito to, 32–33
Fukiage Palace, 187–89
funerals: of Emperor Meiji, 20–21; of Emperor Shōwa (Hirohito), 3–6; of Emperor Taishō, 4

George V, 30, 31, 32

Germany, 25, 97–99, 100–102, 104–5
Gotō, Fumio, 72
Great Kanto Earthquake of 1923, 40
Guadalcanal, 116, 117

Hara, Takashi, 27, 28–29, 35–37, 53
Higashikuni, Naruhiko, 89, 139, 151
Hiranuma, Kiichirō, 99, 104, 129, 130
Hirohito, Emperor: accession of, 44–46; birth of, 9–10; childhood of, 13–18; children of, 42, 90–94, 119, 179–80; coronation of, 45–46, 54–55; death of, 1–3; during the Occupation, 142–48, 152–63, 167–69; education of, 16–18, 23–25; engagement and marriage of, 26–27, 39–41; European visit of, 28–34, 193–96; fiftieth anniversary of reign of, 204–6; funeral of, 3–6; hobbies of, 84, 95–96; meetings with General MacArthur of, 143–48, 176–77; and military actions in China, 50, 51–53, 56, 57–58, 59, 82, 83–86, 88–89; naming of, 10; personal characteristics of, 15–16, 18, 23, 24, 39, 95–96, 159; and Sino-Japanese War (1894–95), 50, 51–53; as regent, 35–37; tours of Japan by, 159–63, 189–91, 207; views of on the imperial system, 67, 165, 203–4; views of on war, 32–33, 58;

visit to the United States of, 196–99, 200–201; and World War II, 5–6, 101–2, 105–9, 111–12, 116–17, 125, 126, 129–36, 147–48, 157–59, 168–74, 201, 205–6, 208–9
Hiroshima, 127, 201–2
Hisa Sachiko, Princess, 90
Hitachi, Prince, 93
Hitler, Adolf, 97, 99, 105, 118, 161
Honjō, Shigeru, 72, 74, 77

Imperial Household Agency, 70, 170, 176, 187, 197, 202, 207–8
Imperial Household Ministry, 38, 61, 153, 170
imperial regalia, 28, 44–45, 123
Imperial Rescript to Soldiers and Sailors, 49
imperial system, 65–67, 156–57, 164–68, 203–4
Indochina, 101–3, 105
Inoue, Junnosuke, 63
International Military Tribunal of the Far East, 62, 162, 169–73, 208
Inukai, Tsuyoshi, 53, 63–64
Ise, Grand Shrine at, 123, 153, 197
Ishiwara, Kanji, 56, 60
Itagaki, Seishirō, 86, 98
Itagaki, Taisuke, 56, 60
Italy, 97–98

kamikaze attacks, 116
Kawamura, Sumiyoshi, 14–15
Kawashima, Yoshiyuki, 72–73, 104
Keenan, Joseph, 169–71

213

Kido, Kōichi, 75, 93, 98, 107, 110, 111, 129, 142, 149, 151, 165–66, 170
Kikuchi, Takeo, 66
Kita, Ikki, 74
Koizumi, Shinzō, 184
Konoe Fumimaro, 86–87, 105, 110, 125–26, 149–50, 168
Korea, 11, 12, 29, 59
Kuni, Prince Kuniyoshi, 26–27, 39, 53–54
Kuomintang, 49, 83
Kurihara, Yasuhide, 69, 71, 77
Kuril Islands, 126, 190
Kwantung Army, 51, 56, 81, 87–89, 127, 171–72

League of Nations, 58–59
Lytton Commission, 59

MacArthur, Douglas, 117, 140, 142–48, 166, 168–69, 175–78
Makino, Nobuaki, 70, 71, 90–91
Manchukuo, 59, 60–62, 87
Manchuria, 12, 49–53, 55–62, 87, 127
Manchurian Incident, 55–56
Matsudaira, Yasumasa, 170, 171
Matsuoka, Yōsuke, 60, 101, 104
May 15 Incident, 63–64
Meiji, Emperor, 18–21, 23, 44, 91, 109, 206
Meiji Constitution, 52–53, 65, 128
Mibuchi, Shigeru, 173
Michiko, Empress. See Shōda, Michiko
Michinomiya. See Hirohito, Emperor

Midway, Battle of, 116
militarism, 49, 53, 63–65, 100, 105
Minobe, Ryōkichi, 205
Minobe, Tatsukichi, 65–68
Mori, Takeshi, 135
Morioka, Yasuhiko, 2–3
Mukden, 55–56

Nagako, Empress, 26–27, 39–41, 92, 94, 95–96
Nagasaki, 127
Nakamura, Shigeru, 78
Nanbara, Shigeru, 173–74
Nashimoto, Morimasa, 149, 150
Nine-Power Pact, 56
Nogi, Maresuke, 16–18, 21–22
Nomonhan Incident, 97–89
Nonaka, Shirō, 69, 78
North China Occupation Army, 81–82
Nosaka, Sanzō, 150

Occupation, Allied, 140–41, 150–52, 164
Oikawa, Koshirō, 108
Okada, Keisuke, 70, 71
Okinawa, 118, 125, 190–91
Okumura, Katsuzō, 145, 147–48
Ōshima, Hiroshi, 98

Pacific War, 113–19
palace, 120–23, 187–89; volunteer grounds maintenance groups at the, 153–56
Pearl Harbor, 113–15
Peers' School, 16–18
Potsdam Declaration, 121, 126–27, 128–31, 140, 203–4

press conferences, 200-4
Pu Yi, 59, 60-62

Ridgway, Matthew, 178
Russia, 12-13. *See also* Soviet Union
Russo-Japanese War, 11-13

Sadako, Empress, 9, 29, 35, 36
Saionji, Kinmochi, 38-39, 53, 64, 90-91, 94
Saipan, 116, 117
Saitō, Makoto, 70, 71
Shidehara, Kijurō, 151-52, 158, 167
Shigemitsu, Mamoru, 57, 75, 140, 147
Shinto, 122, 157, 186
Shirakawa, Yoshinori, 57-58
Shōda, Michiko, 184-86
Shōwa Emperor. *See* Hirohito, Emperor
Shōwa era, choice of name for, 45
"Shōwa Restoration," 69, 70
Sino-Japanese War (1894-95), 11
Sino-Japanese War (1937-45), 81-89, 102-4. *See also* World War II
Soviet Union, 84-85, 87-89, 98, 104-5, 125-26, 127, 171, 172, 177. *See also* Russia
Suga Takako, Princess, 93
Sugiura, Shigetake, 24-25
Sugiyama, Gen, 82-83, 104, 106-7
Suzuki, Kantarō, 52, 70, 71, 125, 126-27, 128-30, 133, 139
Suzuki, Kisaburō, 66, 68

Taishō, Emperor, 4, 21, 28, 35-37, 42-44, 91
Takahashi, Korekiyo, 70, 71
Taka Kazuko, Princess, 90
Takamatsu, Prince, 92
Tanaka, Giichi, 50, 52, 79, 104
Tanaka, Seiichi, 135, 136
Teru Shigeko, Princess, 42, 90, 119, 139
Tōgō, Heihachirō, 24
Tōgō, Shigenori 127, 128, 130
Tōjō, Hideki, 81, 101, 110-11, 124-25, 141-42, 170-71
Tokyo, bombing of, 115-16, 118-20, 124
Tripartite Alliance, 97-99, 101-3, 104

United States of America: 97, 101-3, 105-110, 114; visit of Emperor Hirohito to, 196-99
Usami, Takeshi, 186, 197, 201-2, 204

Vining, Elizabeth, 180-81

war criminals, 56, 141-42, 149-50, 169-70
Watanabe, Jōtarō, 71
World War I, 25
World War II: in Europe, 99, 100-101; in Indochina, 101-3; Japanese surrender in, 128-34, 140; in the Pacific, 113-19. *See also* Sino-Japanese War (1937-45)

Yamagata, Aritomo, 26, 27, 39-40, 53
Yamashita, Tomoyuki, 73, 77

Yasukawa, Takeshi, 197–98
Yasukuni Shrine, 57–58, 208
Yonai, Mitsumasa, 111, 166
Yori Atsuko, Princess, 90
Yoshida, Shigeru, 143, 151, 166
Yoshihito, Emperor. *See* Taishō,
  Emperor